The Secret of the Blue Lotus

Poetry
By
Muata Ashby

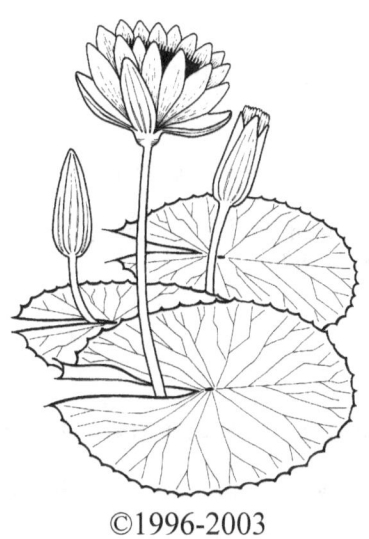

©1996-2003

Cruzian Mystic Books/Sema Institute of Yoga
P.O.Box 570459
Miami, Florida, 33257
(305) 378-6253 Fax: (305) 378-6253

First U.S. edition 1996
Compilation U.S. edition © 2003 By Muata Abhaya Ashby

All rights reserved. No part of this book may be used or reproduced in any manner whatsoever without written permission (address above) except in the case of brief quotations embodied in critical articles and reviews. All inquiries may be addressed to the address above.

The author is available for group lectures and individual counseling. For further information contact the publisher.

Ashby, Muata
The Secret of the Blooming Lotus ISBN: 9781884564161

Library of Congress Cataloging in Publication Data

1 Ancient Egyptian Theater, 2 Egyptian Mythology 3 Spirituality 4 Religion 5 Yoga 6 Self Help.

Other book by Muata Ashby

See back section for more listings.

The Secret Lotus

Poetry of Enlightenment

*by
Muata Ashby*

ABOUT THE AUTHOR

Reginald Muata Ashby D. D., P.C., Y. U.

Reginald Muata Ashby was born in New York City but grew up in the Caribbean. Displaying an early interest in ancient civilizations and the Humanities, he began to study these subjects while in college but put these aside to work in the business world. After successfully running a business with his wife for several years they decided to pursue a deeper movement in life. Mr. Ashby began studies in the area of religion and philosophy and achieved doctorates in these areas while at the same time he began to collect his research into what would later become several books on the subject of the origins of Yoga Philosophy and practice in ancient Africa (Ancient Egypt) and also the origins of Christian Mysticism in Ancient Egypt.

Sema Institute of Yoga/Cruzian Mystic Books P. O. Box 570459 Miami, Florida, 33257
(305) 378-6253 Fax: (305) 378-6253

Oh My Self

When I think of the world do I think of you?
How can I? yet how can I not?

Aren't you everywhere? Or are you only in the present?

I am truly fooled if I know these things not.
I am only a stone, a cloud, an idle piece of glass if I know these things not.

Yet you have always been there, touching me.
Your tenderness always caressing me.

Unfailing in your patience and silence.
You have waited for me always.

Oh my self,
Allow me to become intoxicated with your charm, your very being.

For I can hardly hold back the tears of bliss at the very thought of you.

Oh myself..

Victory

My dearest, my very being, how can I express myself with words. What you are to me, your deepest self is more than any language could convey, any metaphor, any picture.

I could say that you are my most prized possession, the object of my never-ending desire, the very reason of my being, the fire of my existence.

But these small statements would not be true in any way. Because you are more than these.

You are fuller than the eternity of the cosmos. It is in you.

Even the beauty of the most glorious sunset pales in comparison to you. The magnificence of Creation is only a small part of you.

How can I describe the ecstasy of your touch?
The rapture when I think of our encounters?

I could not love you because love is not able to sustain my feeling for you.
So boundless it is.

Having seen you naked in all of your magnificence. Your highest gift I have received.

Now I understand, all things which you are, that I am.

When we appear to be far distant, we are in reality never more distant than a single thought.

The sweetest memories of my existence are incomprehensible when I recall the power of our embrace. So vast you are, so warm and real.

I cannot say that anything else exists, having known you.

Not possible is it for me to know anything else but you.

We are beyond separation and togetherness you and I...
From eternity we have been and for all eternity shall we be.

How do I know you are real? I see you and yet do not know your form. I cannot touch you but yet I can feel you.

I must lose myself in you, then I know what is real.

Oh... would everyone know you, the peace that you are, the comfort.
May they live in you as I do.

I know nothing else of you. Nothing else do I need to know.

How can I show you my feeling, to you who are everything? You who are the feeling in my heart.

What can I give to you who are everything, you who have given so much, you who are all there is to give and receive.

Not less than All that I am can it be.
All giving to All.

That is what you are to me.

The Goal

...through study, reflection, meditation and order and right action, love, wisdom, divine adoration, harmony, cultivation of the powers of the spirit,

You will know and experience the truth,

You will achieve supreme peace and stability...
to know thyself... In this, the greatest human task,
You will discover who you are.
You will know that there is only one consciousness that exists, it is yours.
You will discover that all that exists depends on your consciousness.
You will know that your consciousness is the same one, which underlies and supports all other human beings.

Further, you will know that this consciousness is distinct from the mortal, ego-personality of others, that it is their true inner self, their soul, of which even they are unaware, your soul is one with every other soul.

Finally, You will discover unbounded peace in knowing you are immortal. The greatest enemies of humanity: ignorance and egoism will be banished from your consciousness.

You have unified the opposites into one whole, you have achieved control over your intellect, you have created your own supreme divine destiny, you have achieved all there is to achieve, you know all there is to know, you are one with all things.

You have achieved the supreme good. You will live eternally in your eternal-glorious-spiritual body. This is steadfastness, your true divine essence.

Your soul is one with the Universal Soul, GOD, The Hidden One, the one who is beyond thought, who is the indwelling essence of all things, this is who you really are! To know oneself is to know GOD!

Oh God!

"Adorations"

How many times have you spoken of the subtlety of the mind, the illusoriness of the world process, the oneness of creation and such things?
For years has it been or since the beginning of time?...

How is it possible to express appreciation for one such as you....
Could words suffice? could any gift the fullness of feeling hold or express?...

Would every breath , every step, every moment of conscious devotion sufficient be?
Otherwise it could not be since every breath, every step and all consciousness you are...

Receiving of the gift of pearls with true reverence, listening and reflecting constantly, doing one's best to achieve yoga...
A greater show of appreciation could there be?...

Somehow, with your illumination, the pain and disappointment of life turn into to desire for freedom and understanding...

Then the moment unobstructed, unveils its precious gifts... time and space give way to eternity and infinity ... the enigmatic smile of the Buddha becomes intelligible... the mysteries, the joys and sorrows of life, a jungle of sorrow and bewilderment, no longer are they...

But a spectacle of magic to dance with...

A great blessing it is in deed, to be in your company... for everywhere you are...
In the cacophony of life as well as the stillness of supreme peace...

In the heights of the universe but never farther away than one's very self, the heart of hearts...

To share in you, would that all may be blessed!

Adorations to you in the sun!...
Adorations to you in the distant stars!...
Adorations to you in the seed of the humble grass!...
Adorations to you who dwell in the heart of all things!...

Adorations! Adorations!

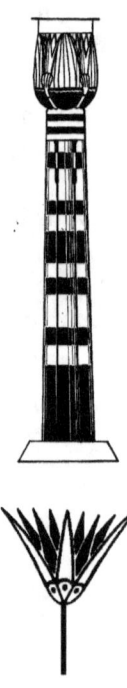

The Mirror

Today I have realized I am just a mirror,
I looked around men and in all directions I could find nothing real.

Many thoughts and ideas of great plans and deeds to come but still nothing real.

Then I looked again and I saw you.
And at once I realized I was just a mirror.

A reflection of glory and infinity was I.
For all the things I could say or do, there were no words to express the feeling of your sight.

All I can say is that I am just a mirror.
And the mirror is not real.

But the mirror reflects the glory incomparable and the bliss beyond words.

Oh... I am just a mirror.

I Am Silence

I tried, long and hard but then it was so simple.
To find a way to see you, to find you, to know you.

How could I know, how could anyone know the way.
There are so many trees, canyons and abysses to traverse.

But among them all there you are.
So simple, so close and yet so far.

I realized I could not find you.
Nothing I could do would help.

Because you are silence and silence is your way.

When I was tired of trying, desperate and in dire need I became silent.

And in silence I saw you and I can no longer share in the noise of existence.

For that noise is not silence.

I am silence with you.

The Exalted Feeling

The exalted feeling is here today, once again with the message of bliss.

As if from nowhere but from everywhere it comes.

Bringing with it the beauty of being.

The exalted feeling is my deepest self.
Let me know it fully and allow me to abide there always.

The exalted feeling is all there is.
How can there be more than what is?

When everything touched, felt, seen or thought gives the exalted feeling, then I know I am home.

I am the exalted feeling...

Look at Me

Look at me and what is there?
Am I what you see or am I the fruit of what cannot be seen.

Am I the frailty, the solid object of perception or am I something else...

Look at me and see yourself.
For I am the fullness of being.

In me there are mountains and galaxies which span the vast imagination and abide in what is real in me.

But I am no different than you.
When I look at you I see an endless ocean of vastness.

For we are the same, you and I.

Isn't everything?

I am Nothing

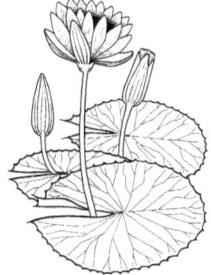

All the desires, all of the fears, all of the reasons, all of the energy, seeking, wanting, needing.

And alas what am I?

Nothing can be said, nothing denied for having looked into the world I find I am not there.

Where am I then? Who am I then? or whatever?
I am nothing there, nor here am I.

Care for nothing because there is nothing to care for.
Search for nothing for there is nothing to search for.
Feel for nothing for there is nothing to feel for, yet I am.

Doing yet for no reason, only being am I.
I am being, being itself and being is not feeling nor wanting nor needing yet it is all of these as well.

Therefore I am nothing, nothing of here, nothing of acquaintance or possession or desire.

I am nothing yet I go on, and as I become more nothing I am more neutral yet more intimate for separation and being nothing is knowing deeply.

Essence I am but nothing of this yet All I am, yet nothing of this.

Therefore, take me more and do as you need for I am nothing of this, yet I am All.

Care not yet caring is, need not for fulfillment is always there, doing much yet devoid of desire.

Where does it come from? It is you for I am nothing of this.

It is you who are doing and you alone who know for I am nothing of this and yet I am All in you.

You are my dream

More and more I peer into the darkness...and the more I do, I see that the light is an illusion.

This glorious dream is all around and in everything and who knows its true nature?

This dream is full of partners and others, happenings and great expectations yet it is only a dream.

A tremendous dream yet only a dream.

I see your reflection in every part of this dream and yet it is only a reflection.

A glorious reflection yet only a reflection.

This dream breathing, walking, seeing, touching, smelling, tasting is the reflection of you who are being.

Always dancing with me I need no other partner,
Always breathing for me I need not seek breath,
Always seeing for me, I need not look anywhere for you are my dream, And the dream is continuous, full and eternal as you are as I am.

You are my dream and I am yours, for how much longer?

Shall we not meet again and dance the dance of my destruction,
Oh allow me to be destroyed again and again in your arms.
For when I am destroyed I am full and this is the realization of you who are my dream.

Let us dream on the dream of eternity and let us dance the dance of my destruction for when I am destroyed I am full, oh so full.

What else do I know?
You are my dream and this I know...

Let us dream on the dream of eternity and let us dance the dance of my destruction for when I am destroyed I am full oh so full...

A Trip to the Sun

Where have I gone, to the sun of splendorous essence.

With waves of iridescent blue and white.

Waves of glory and ice and fire. Waves of misty essence and welcoming coolness.

Hanging there in the vast ocean of space like a milky cloud of radiating splendor.

So inviting and so lustrous, welcoming in to the heart, the core, the soul of true splendor.

And what splendors were there, what wondrous beauty which defies description were seen there.

Oh what splendors and beauties which cannot be described in words or thoughts these.

To be experienced only are they, for experience is true knowing and true understanding.

Therefore go there, to the sun and be the sun, be as you are in your heart.

Be the sun.

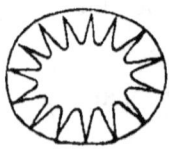

The Glimpse

For an instant it was, that time stood still.
For an instant it was truth alone that was.

In that instant all that was to be known was, and all that could be known also was.

This instant occurred in a glimpse and the glimpse was for all eternity and in eternity.

Becoming the source of absolute oneness, beyond oneness, incomprehensible yet all knowing.

The source of all that is, was and to be, in the glimpse.

The glimpse reveals that I am the source, that all things come from me and that everyone, like me is also the source.

Not the me that you can see but the innermost me which is the innermost you.

May you be granted the grace of a glimpse such as this for this kind of glimpse is no glimpse but a truth.

A truth which dissolves the mystery of thought.
A moment out of time and space into a realm divine.

Gaze into the timeless realm and behold immortality and eternity in a flash.

The glimpse reveals that the world is not real, nor the one glimpsing nor the glimpse itself.

But it reveals the source of truth and the source of reality and the world is a reflection of that source.

Therefore, is the reflection not as real as the source? Is the image in the mirror as real as the source of the reflection?

Why to be immersed in the reflection and not in the source?

Therefore take a glimpse and go to the source.

Watch the world as it dissolves before you as a dream melts with the dawn of awakening.

This glimpse is the last of the world you will see for all else to come in the world is lesser than this. There is nothing else to see in the world for there is no world, no reality but the view from the glimpse.

The temporal is a dream from the timeless viewpoint of the Glimpse and why indulge in a dream?

Therefore, take a glimpse and go to the source.
The source of all things is in the heart.

Flying

How is it, taking flight?
How is it, waking up?

How does it feel to be free of the body?
How does it feel to be free of all weight, all concern, and all strife?

Go flying and discover bliss, this world of bodies is felling to the real you, therefore, go flying and discover bliss.

Be still and take flight and be free from the illusion of body.

Be still and take flight and discover you can fly.

Across the universe to the Holy Lands to the stars, discover you can fly and in flight drink the nectar of bliss.

Move forth through the fear of bottomless falling, there is nowhere to fall but into your own blessed arms...for you are the blessed mother who watches after her children and breaks the fall into the gentle clouds of serenity after the storm.

The storm is the world, the storm is the mind and it's ignorance and fear of flying.

Therefore, face the fear, take flight.
For the rewards are bliss and knowing.

Bliss and knowing, greater gifts than these are not to be found except by facing fear and taking flight.

Therefore, give up fear, which keeps you immersed in ignorance, disheartened, dispirited and weighed down.

Therefore, face the fear, take flight.
For the rewards are bliss and knowing.

Just be still, face fear, take flight and discover you can fly.

The Absolute

I have learned so much about you.

The sciences of today and the myths of ancient times tell of you but they also say that there is a mystery that goes beyond their words.

Science has examined the smaller and larger parts of you and there is infinity in both.

Science has examined your body and found not matter but energy and transcendence beyond what is knowable by science.

But the ancient mystics had said this from time immemorial, that this world is nothing but a subtle manifestation of your mind.

Oh Hidden Absolute One, as you grace this creation with your being and shower over all with the nectar of existence and sustenance I am blessed to know you.

While hidden you are everywhere and in all things and thus being you are absolute and singular.

As you are singular I am also singular and all that is, is singular in you.

Thus, I am bliss Absolute, the hidden essence of all that is.

There is no here and there, you and me nor question nor answer nor craving or need, no inner nor outer.

Only oneness and no thought besides...this is being Absolute and One.

Thus, I am the inner and the outer as I am one with you who are the essence of all inner and outer things.

Enfolded and circumscribed in the Hidden Absolute am I... are you.

Taking Flight

Have you ever taken flight?

Have you found that place within yourself which is beyond thoughts?

That place of purity and clarity.
That place where freedom reigns.

Go there right now and I will meet you there.

We will take flight and explore this wondrous land of ours – the universe.
We will explore our vastness, our majesty, our infinity!

Not bound are we to our physical form unless we want to be.
Supremely free are we when we find that place – sacred in our hearts.

Now that you know me will you ever leave me?

I am the supreme abode of all that you are, have been and will be.
Come to me and I will give you refuge forever.

Shelter you from any harm, pain and sorrow.
This I will do for you by your mere request.

Therefore, come to me and never fear.
For I have provided you with all things.

Can you feel me now?

I never left you, but you left me, to marvel in strange lands.

Can you remember me now?

Exhilaration

Tonight I have been given a gift.

Your divine touch has lifted the weight of the world from my shoulders.
Though I find myself in a lowly place, in the company of strangers and relatives.

I am exhilarated by your touch…
When you touch me I feel nothing else.

Nor can I think of anything else.
When you touch me I am one with you, there is no longer me.

How can I explain the desire to lose myself in you?
To forget whatever I am doing, whatever I am or was?

Maybe it is because when you touch me I somehow know that I am really you.
That I exist by your will.

That at the deepest level I am really you and you are me.

Oh God!

You are exhilaration when you touch me…I am that too.

The Storm

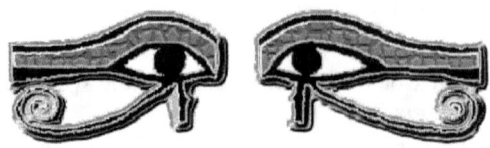

What is a storm?

I am a storm and so are you.

As we flow through the changes of life, through the turmoils of childhood, youth and old age we are storms stirring up the waters

What are the waters, these?

The waters of the mind.

From the calmness of sleep there is the stirring up of awakening.

And where does this stirring up lead us?

Sometimes to happiness and sometimes to sorrow seldom to peace.

And anything that is not peace is a storm.

Therefore I say:
I am a storm and so are you.

But how can this be, how can we be of two natures and yet somehow different, special, transcendental?

In a storm there is a whirling rage and at the center a still calm.
Is there not peace and the storm within us at the same time?

For the more I see the storm the more I see emptiness and when I look upon the storm with deep concern I see less and less substance.

Less in the storm and more in you and me.

So perhaps when we see beyond the storm we may find each other though not feeling, hearing or seeing, but in knowing...

For I am not the storm but the peace and so are you.

The Dream

What is the dream?

The dream is that of me which you see.

How do you know me? From the sight, the touch, the smell, the hearing?

These things myself are not. For that which you see is the dream.

The dream is waking up, going to sleep and hoping, and longing, and wanting.

The dream is all of these things for these do not last and dreams do not last.

So what is it of me which you see? It is the dream, It is the dream.

What you see is imperfection and perfection; a mixture of these is what you see of me and I of you.

How can these be seen together? Can water and Oil be seen together?

There is a fault somewhere... in what we see, feel, hear, touch or smell.

Where is the fault?

It is in dreaming, in the dreaming...

So wake me up from the dream of the dreaming and let me know what is not the dreaming.

That which is not the dreaming is timeless and eternal, to be known with the heart.

Where is this knowing which comes from the heart? It is not in the dreaming therefore wake up and see what is to be known with the heart.

Leave what you see, feel, hear, touch and smell and then know with the heart.

This is the waking from the dream.

The Road Home

The road home is before me.
With every breath it extols the heart of me.

Beckoning to follow the twists and turns.
Challenging the one who is homeward bound.

The ups and downs are long and treacherous and many times
fallen am I on the road.

This falling is a luminous rising.
This falling is a grounding of thought.
This falling is a time of deep feeling.
This falling is for me the road home.

Falling on the road is following the road.
For the road is everywhere when a deepening, grounding thought
arises.

Therefore, my falling is my following.
My falling is the discovery of the road home.

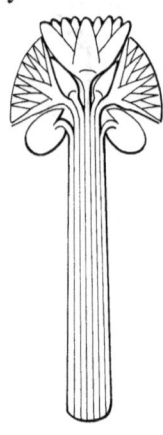

Can you feel me now?

Can you feel me now?
So many years I have waited.
So many times of trials, and despair.

But I never left you even when you ignored me.

Can you feel me now?

I am at the very heart of you and always was.
Waiting, longing for your company.

But so many times you left me, so many times you went seeking for another.

And in so many ways you forsook me but I was always there.

Can you feel me now?

So close and never farther away than a thought.

Can you feel me now?
What do you need for I am here?

Look anywhere and I am there.
Touch anything and I am there.
Listen to everything and I am there.
Taste anything and I am there.
Smell anything and I am there.

But mostly think anything and I am there. Know something and I am known, know nothing and I am known.

Can you feel me now?
Are all these things not you?

Can you feel me now? Can you feel you?

Illusions divorce

Nothing more do I want with you, O illusion.

What have you brought me but longing, and desire for things, which never sufficed, things that brought more longing?

Therefore I divorce you O illusion, for I have traveled the winding trails of your whispers and urges to move on and seek to find what is sufficient.

And sufficient it is not what I have found with you nor could ever be for illusion is not sufficient nor could ever be.

Thus I divorce you O illusion and for whom do you say?

I leave you for the real, the abiding, that which is cooling.

Are you cooling, abiding, real and what then are these things?

I am these things and more for I have discovered your illusion.

Who or what are you O illusion? Where can I find you? Who wants you?

For the love of the real there are those who get you. But what do they get but illusion.

How did I discover you? I discovered that I too was an illusion so I left you and myself.

For to know you is knowing illusoriness and illusoriness alone can know illusion thus illusoriness gone so are your illusions, thus illusoriness gone so is me and my and I.

And with both of us gone all there is left is the real...

A Song of Love

With this song I think of unrequited love.

What is love?
I can find love in anything I see.

I am alone.
But it has always been so.

And yet there is a familiarity with the lack of love.

A memory, a kinship.

And I give myself to this lack of love, and feeling what do I know?

I know that what I seek I cannot find, nor feel nor see.

I cannot see what is not real.
And I cannot see myself in all that I see.

And yet I am and I love.

I know I cannot find what I already have.

Because I am love and love is,
Not there but here.

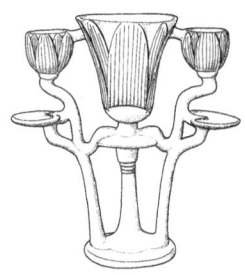

Your Ups and Downs

I can see you in your ups and downs.

But I can no longer touch you nor can I express feeling to you.

Feeling escapes me and I do not know this wave that I see.

The surge surges on and life brings more ups and downs.

And I see you as I drift farther away and I reach for you with my body;
yet I know I cannot touch you.

So I am paralyzed even though we move about,
we see and touch but there is no way.

When will the gap close between us?
Can it close when it does not even exist?

I am so paralyzed, beyond lifting a thought,
Because there is no place to reach for, there is no use reaching.

I cannot touch what I see because it is untouchable as the fleeting ray of the sun.

I cannot touch what I see because what I see is only your reflection.

Hold you in my arms I cannot.

But there is a place where I hold you,
but even there I cannot touch,
that place in me,
that place is you,
that place is all.

So let me see how beautiful you are I me.

When I see you I see my glory,
and you can see my glory through you.

So let me never touch,
never seek,
never want.
Prevent my attempts, for as I am deprived I drink the nectar of bliss.

Oh Lady of Glories

Oh Lady of Glories!
Awaken your fierce nature.

I await you eagerly.
I await your presence.

I offer this child as the canvas of your work.

May you mold and burn this aggregate of elements.
May you have your way as an insistent mother who is caring and wise.

Cause the pain and consume the darkness.

Carry me to the height of heights.

Oh Divine Mother.

Enfold me as only you can,
and never let me go.

Never let me go for I am the heart of your essence.

Carry me away on the journey of journeys.

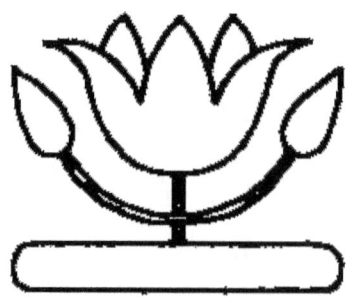

The Glow

Shower me, Shower me! The Flow of Sap upon the tree.

Intoxicated with glow for no where has the flow to go,
But upwards and downwards and sidewards and allwards.

Oh glow, You are enjoyed but not held,
Felt but not coveted,

Oh Glow, Shower me, Shower me.

How can you be if another is not present?
Can it be that another need not be?
Or can it be that another is here in you?

Oh Glow, Shower me, Shower me.

Intoxicating is your touch,
Overwhelming is your embrace,
Like a slow burning ember,
Like a fragrant scent of bliss,
Like a nectarine solution of peace and joy!

Oh Glow, Shower me, Shower me.

Wherefore glow on, like a secret confection of heaven.
And I will keep the secret of your flow. So flow on, Oh Glow, flow on.

For your pleasure the instrument is yours to ignite,
For your pleasure the instrument is yours to kindle,
For your pleasure the instrument is yours to incinerate,
For your pleasure the instrument is yours to set a blaze!

Oh Glow, Shower Me, Shower me.

Tingle the place where the flow lets go,
Crawl the way, round about for the sake of beatitudes blessed knowing,
Burn your way and hurt the good hurt,
For you shower me all over, Glow on Glow on,
Forever and ever more.

The Illusions I Created

What is this life that I made for myself?
The career, the job, the family the history?
All that I care for, all that I believe in?
What is this life and that which is so important?
Whence did it begin and whence will it end?

What do I know of these, and what do they know of me?
That which I loved that was so dear and quaint,
Such that was clean and pure for sake of desire,
Lo, I hear the call of these, but what do they know of me and me of them?

They tell me in subtle ways, in harsh ways and quaint ways,
But I do not listen to the sounds of disappointment,
I do not listen to the sounds of frustration,
For the sake of desire and passion I move forward, forgetful and blind.

When I am deaf to the sound of their pleading,
They push upon me the pain that wakes up the blunted mind.

They tell me that they are the illusions I have created,
They tell me sweet whispers of truth I cannot bear.

Hurtful are the truths of the illusions I have created,
Challenging me to see beyond the mist of my own fancy.

What is there for me if I listen to their words?
Am I to be ever lost in the sea of created illusions?

Oh this is hard,
The choice of giving up all!
For I cannot ignore the truth of my illusions.

As I leave my illusions,
The illusions I have created,
I wander in the sea of truth and the beyond.

My illusions were real,
But a reality based on illusion.
And a reality of illusion is nothing more than a neat prison of my own creation.

The illusions of my own creation take me away from truth,
The illusions of my own creation take me away from peace.

So let me leave the illusions of my creation,
And let me experience the truth of letting go.
For there is no greater pain than the illusion,
The illusion which is of one's very own creation.

And there is no greater happiness than discovering,
The illusion of the illusions of my creation.

What Has Been Said?

Oh tell me will you what has been said?
I wander around this place of longing and loss of head.

Where is there to go, what is their to say?
The speaking is up and the understanding is played.

Over and over with so many turns.
Running as if on a treadmill which a hamster learns.

Oh go somewhere and do something you will this very today.
And whatever I have done, tomorrow will wither and decay.

For I no longer forget the pain of doing and yet not doing is the fates.
Of all who seek to know the cause of doings ravaging, move towards the pearly gates.

Understanding is as understanding does.
And there is no understanding since there never was any cause.

For what you see is not doing but a feeling blowing in the wind.
And time all blows and doing flies away to the place where all believe they can the price win.

Try again and see how I beat you down,
And you will know finally how to wear the crown.

Tell me all that I wish to know,
And I will see your everlasting glow,
For I am not the one whose words are failing,
It is you, the vast world who have taken the speech for nibbling.

All I asked for was a place to sit,
And you refused me even an inch of a tiny splint.
For what reason this cruelty and hardness?

Oh it is my own need to receive, to have that luxury and fullness!

So it was me, all along, the foe and the master.
But even these words cannot ever hope to capture,
The story of wind and the pain of discovering nothing,
Or the feeling of love and the fruit of understanding?

Bitter-sweet indeed is your message,
And I hold no hope to surpass your tidings which are certainly blessed.

I Am Filled

Filled I am, with what can't be said
Know not yet knowing is the name
Of what I know not where or when
I call to you and you come and fill me again O so again

Filled with you I am and what, who, when can't be said
For I know not where or when but when I call you I am filled again

I cannot move nor can I see for I am filled with you
And you are there when I go to and fro
So here I am filling myself with you again and again
And when I do I am you again
But who am I and who are you?
I know not now, whenever or then
For I am you and filled again and again.

With light and silence I am filled again
Speaking not, for in such there is no gain

Looking not, there is no see to pertain
Hearing not, the hearing is only filling with you again

Allow me to breath again and again
Filling me with you, like the lake, the rain
With light golden and luminous
To the top of me beyond the superfluous

Cannot speak those worlds of praise,
For the feeling cannot any further be raised

In any case the speech is impaired
How can a river flow when a dam has been declared?

Fill me up, dam up the world with your presence
And let me see not, hear not, touch not, except you filling me!

Adorations to the Preceptor

Glories abound in the three worlds but none so sublime as the aspirant finding a teacher.
All the world over there are souls listening to preachers,
But who understands, who is more than just a leacher?

When the student and teacher meet they become like weavers.
Hand in hand they go creating the garment of knowing that cures the world fever.
Disease so great and yet nonexistent.
Knowing the truth by becoming supremely transcendent.

And knowing is grand, all exalted and high.
There is so much knowing in this world and yet the world continues to fly.
Off into delusion, hysteria and pride.
Given over to the fanciful pictures and rides.

Who is that person that goes further than the covers?
Students of teachers sitting on their towers.
Those who yearn and go further they prostrate.
Upon seeing that person who is poised to create.

Worlds within worlds where there previously had been clouds.
Lo, has been engendered the light which all crowds.
Gather around to receive removal of all hindrance.
And knowing upon knowing where there had once been ignorance.

That person cannot be called preceptor for no name can contain the light.
Coming forth from the person, clad in saffron rites.
Glory to you whoever you are.
For I know not your name and yet am blinded by your star.

Essence benign and wise and pure.
Like a magnet are the seekers attracted to you who fore sure.

Leading then you are to that place without name.
Beyond time and space far beyond the earth plane.

To discover glories and bliss absolute.
You have led those who know you by playing your divine flute.
The music of your words is the poetry of the soul.
Which you speak so well as the star shining over your fold.

Like the good shepherd leading the foundlings.
Having lost their way, to safety they are lead rounding.
Avoiding the pitfalls and hurt and grief.
You are the source for all joy eternal and divinity to meet.

Adorations again and a thousand times more.
From a disciple forever and a follower of the ancient lore.
Which purifies and makes holy the student who is your follower.
Always may I be among those at your feet in the precious time
of the lecture hour.

A Thought for the Suffering

Why can't we hear the cries of the suffering?
Until its too late, the internal voice keeps us wondering.

Where to turn and how to find,
redemption's peace and heavens sign.

When the suffering strike out in pain and sorrow,
is revenge the answer to those who are already so low?

The people need, the people cry,
as we look on them and then turn away to pry,

The mighty dollar for life bed and wine,
to be happy here and now to relax and unwind.

But the cries go on, still unheard,
and their lives continue without even a caring word.

A place for pain and frustrations lashes,
has been made for the suffering, teeming masses.

What can they do, unheard and wasted?
Pained by the callous world we have created.

So never should it be wondered how the suffering on us turned,
in the time when it counted we hadn't learned.

To wake us up to our duty to the family of humanity,
and never turn away from the suffering or with charity be untimely.

For the pain of the suffering should be like our own pain,
and never should we rest until suffering is ends claim.

Because where there is suffering, and a blind eye,

there is surely resentment and hatred ready to fly.

And the illusion that there is safety in isolation,
Is quickly disproven by the successful strikes that leave us with a horrible expression.

So whoever you are your suffering, is my responsibility,
if I have hurt you in any way I seek your forgiveness freely.

I for give you for your words and acts of anger,
for these were coming not from the soul but from years of rancor.

And together brother, sister, friend,
we will find the answer to suffering and hatred's end.

If we move in this way of virtue,
we will ultimately find sufferings purpose and path to:

Enlightenment.

The Words of the Teacher

From ancient days, from the time of yore,
it was told to all to heed the secret lore.

Throughout the trials and daunting struggles,
the aspirant is tested, the ordeal of their morals.

And when they seek and find the teachers,
why do they treat them like ordinary preachers?

With words of praise and high admiration,
dropping accolades like rain drops in inundation.

Supporting the impression of true longing,
only to be dashed by the cruel awakening.

That here and now is the time always passing by,
and wasting away without achieving genuine high.

For there is more in aspiring than words and appearance,
there also must be the strictest and faithful adherence,

to the words of the teacher and the glory of the Divine,
that tears asunder the egoistic brine,

so tasty, so satisfying to the palate and the senses,
as deadly and binding to the word that otherwise cleanses,

pure hearts and minds for the journey to the past,
that time when everything was as it will be at the last.

So what to make of these words of the teacher,
Which should be the means to defeat the fear of the fearer,

inside every aspirant who longs for the great release,
but through limitation only finds the path like climbing a pole
with grease.

Morals are judged by deeds the sages have said,
and what curious actions done by people who have only read?

The dutiful listeners must do as they are told,
before the time comes when the swiftest is no match for the bold,

world of illusions which grips and ties,
like the constrictor serpent in certain demise,

those presents given by the world,
to the mistaken, naïve child who believe they can unfurl,

the wings of wisdom without the breeze of Divine Love,
is like the impotent revolt against the clouds above.

And when these two wings of the mind and feeling,
are ready to see the panoramic view of the world fleeting,

the feeble flutter becomes the soaring falcon,
and the blind eye opens the way to the secret passion.

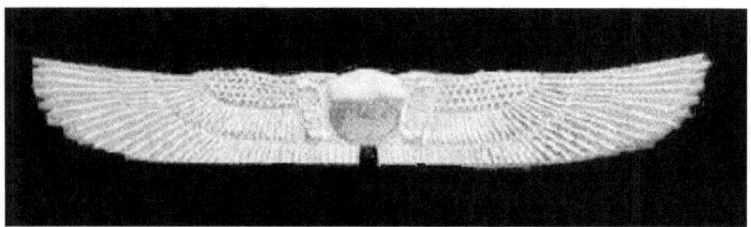

Why listen?

Smelling the incense of fragrance divine,
there is a tendency to look back in foolish repine,

the consequence of actions desired or taken,
as if that would somehow the repercussions lessen.

Oh laugh and cry and in the end what do you achieve?
the satisfaction of crying and tormenting the plebe.

Those high and mighty thoughts of virtue that surprise,
upon unveiling and showing their own arrogance to the pride.

So why listen, and to who listen when listen and where?
there is so much to take in so as not to look square.

For so long I have wandered and so long I have sought,
and what has my exploration led to, what has it wrought?

Look not here for answers since that would be talking,
and talking when listening is like turning on the charm and singing,

praises and glories and homage and roses,
for those who only want to end the pain and losses,

oh world, oh me, oh you and I,
the time has come for the awful reply.

But when there is time to speak there is clinging to old ways,
and never came the words of repentance, faith and no more plays,

for this drama is not and yes it is,
the answer not, can it be just a quiz?

To all who ask the deep questions of life,

and end up holding the bag from misdeeds now ripe,

with quandary and passion and sincerity cometh,
the merry band which life playeth on it.

The desires and expectations are trampled with the music,
and time rolls on and the opportunity of life loses it.

Quiet and listen for the comforting word,
and take the steps that make a sound that was never heard.

Tread the path of triumph and loss,
the overwhelming sound of the crushing boss,

who lords over one who is ignorant and simple,
the world is that lord rolling over the principle,

of taking for granted life's gifts and promise,
and making a mockery of god's plans, the premise,

that I am one you are and it is an all entwined,
come together in time and space all to ultimately unwind,

as the matrix for all that has become and will be,
when will I ever understand and come this to see.

So I listen and quiet in hopes of destroying,
the pester, the phony, the clown come a peering,

into my world of illusion and sorrow,
revealing the truth of life, in reality the unfettered sparrow.

Glory in the little things

The subtle heartbeat so precious and powerful,
allows me to experience god's glory a world brimful.

The sound of a bee and the stirring of morning,
call to waking of mind to the infinite forging,

of life on the move, in all directions and methods,
to let me know the grandeur, of life like strings on levers.

So delicate and mysterious is being and existence,
little is it realized all this happens just for instance.

A miracle, a magical, dance of mirrors,
infinite number of reflections in mind's rivers,

the streams of thought making love to the world,
with the senses touching, the things all a twirl.

Dancing the dance is the touch of the sun,
On my skin are the rays, like children running just for fun.

Where is this place? oh how can I know?,
who cares for this knowledge does it matter is there a foe?

I cherish this place wherever it is,
whether awake or dreaming, I am always a whiz,

at seeing the glory deep down in the center,
at the place where the dancers meet the director,

of life's little glories and sorrows and pleasures,
these and more are life's meaning and measures.

For living and feeling the breezes and noises,
eternal is the magic between time's little poises.

Send me to the place where there is eternal feeling,
In death there not to end, the journey transcending.

For what is there to feel in eternity's bosom,
the laughter of fullness and feeling's fulcrum.

For I am the center, the glory of feeling,
And wherever I may be I am always existing!

The Hell of the Shrewd, The Hell of the Crude

I see hell every day in the eyes of children,
all over the world who have lost their standing in,

societies quest for power and lust,
their eyes have gone cold from the neglect slavery and rust,

of blades and spades thrust deep into their hearts,
by lost souls calling themselves presidents, parents, priests and parts,

of the civilized world which craves for more,
just like the enemy, the terrible infidel of yore.

That enemy over there, the villain, monster and cruel,
if only I had more money to by more of his fuel,

so I could buy bigger cars and strut my stuff,
and make everyone's life in the world a little more ruff.

Cause I see hell over there but not in my own place,
That would be like saying that my life is but a waste.

For my life is very worthy, happy and true,
No matter that I hate myself, my family and you.

Wait just a minute I did not mean to say,
that life is a boring roll in the hey,

I laugh and smile and agree with what you do,
So long as it helps my cause and no trouble will ensue.

And what trouble can come of my arrogance and disdain,
For the world and all its miracles like life, sunshine and rain,

Which come from the heavens and nurture every vine,
That I use for pleasure, entertainment and wine?

Oh yes the world is wonderful, yet I stay within my walls,
With the television turned up loud so I can hear nobody's calls,

From all those who I have made destitute,
Because of my greed and sanctimonious rectitude.

am busy running around from morning till late at night,
Keeping the world the way I want it to stay in sight.

For this illusion always serves my purpose,
To pull the wool over the eyes of those who serve us.

And when we have had our fill of the world and its pleasures,
We start a fight so that nobody will see the levers,

For there is no shortage of grievances against our policies,
The way we control other people's lives with controversies.

Those strings attached to everything we do,
That make everyone around us follow our rule.

Conscience be quiet can't you see,
that I am the master and you are a slave to me.

My cleverness has been monumental,
Even in my own household when my family tells me I am mental.

I lord over the world and control all the finances,
And low and behold I do not understand why the flame dances,

As a molotov cocktail burns my house up in a fit of rage,
Because I was never there when my teenager went to a rave.

Now they have all left me, alone and forlorn,

On my deathbed all I bequeath is pettiness and scorn,

I leave vices, bitterness and regrets for posterity,
so that my children will carry on creating more money.

For if my life is worth nothing in virtue,
can't it surely be valued in some sort of revenue?

Is this not the way that I learned while young?
that the meaning of life is measured by a person's corporate rung?

Survival of the fittest is the law of the jungle,
and the world be dammed because I am master of the juggle.

That skillful art of scheme and deception,
Where I tell myself I am the greatest and then you give me an ovation.

I see the hell over there and within me,
This is why I can't bear you to be one with thee.

My toys and gadgets keep me distracted,
To the world we live in which I withheld wealth from, protracted.

Miserable is life, for men, women, girls and boys,
they never promised us a rose garden, just the choice of righteousness or ploys.

And so I'm not so bad after all,
As long as I live as a queen and never bee seen to crawl.

And even as my illusions begin to shatter,
 I will build a bigger wall, wave my flag and get fatter.

So that through the fog of my own chronic wheeze,
I will be insulated from all of the desperate pleas.

And this is the hell both at the top and the bottom,
for the haves who have all and the have nots with no forum.

The End

        The end, the end, the end is coming,
        The end, the end, the end is near.

I fought, the fight, and lost the battle,
the view, the day, was always clear.

I never knew, the heights of sorrow,
the plan, was all, deluded fears.

        The end, the end, the end is coming,
        The end, the end, the end is near.

Come see, come hear, the mighty vision.
Crash down, along, with glorious dreams.

I went, so far, and saw so little.
The great, the small, came down with me.

        The end, the end, the end is coming,
        The end, the end, the end is near.

Hail all, the world, and all its beauty.
Bow down, to all, illusions found.

I'm free, today, forget tomorrow.
Tomo'rrows ne'ver come to me.

        The end, the end, the end is coming,
        The end, the end, the end is near.

Hey can, you hear, the awful calling?
Hey can, you see, the marvel dawning?

Of peace, of calm, that's in the ending.

So look, here now, the end is coming.

Hail all, come around, the end is near.

Salute, the pride, and bid farewell,
to all, desire futile claim.

> Hey… the end, the end, the end is coming,
> The end, the end, the end is near.
>
> The end, the end, the end is coming,
> The end, the end, the end is near….

Fire and Rain

       I've seen fire and rain.
       Oh I've known glory and pain.

Forever, whenever I see a smile on a child.
I know that's the clever, play time of the divine.

       I've seen fire and rain.
       Oh I've known glory and pain.

Forever, whenever, I see hunger on the face of life.
I know that's the center, of ego's high on the wine.

       I've seen fire and rain.
       Oh I've known glory and pain.

You… you… have seen the cries of the child.
This… this… is pain from the guns all the while.

You… you…have seen the fears of the child.
This… is insane, the hunger of greed all the while.

       I've seen fire and rain.
       Oh I've known glory and pain.

       I've seen fire and rain.
       Oh I've known glory and pain.

Ra….Ra….sees all the pain.
Never believe this is all in vain.

I know the humor of life in time.
So I don't believe in the culture of crime.

       I've seen fire and rain.
       Oh I've known glory and pain.

Save me, save the child,
                    He's the heart of your soul.

No matter who you are,
                    The fight for truth is never old.

Save me, save the child,
                    She's the heart of your soul.

Fight the power of darkness,
                    Virtue is so bold.

Love me, I am the child,
                    Of your heart and soul.

Never, Never let my story be untold!

All you do is say:

        I've seen fire and rain.
        Oh I've known glory and pain.

Why listen?

Smelling the incense of fragrance divine,
there is a tendency to look back in foolish repine,

the consequence of actions desired or taken,
as if that would somehow the repercussions lessen.

Oh laugh and cry and in the end what do you achieve?
the satisfaction of crying and tormenting the plebe.

Those high and mighty thoughts of virtue that surprise,
upon unveiling and showing their own arrogance to the pride.

So why listen, and to who listen when listen and where?
there is so much o take in so as not to look square.

For so long I have wandered and so long I have sought,
and what has my exploration led to, what has it wrought?

Look not here for answers since that would be talking,
and talking when listening is like turning on the charm and singing,

praises and glories and homage and roses,
for those who only want to end the pain and losses,

oh world, oh me, oh you and I,
the time has come for the awful reply.

But when there is time to speak there is clinging to old ways,
and never came the words of repentance, faith and no more plays,

for this drama is not and yes it is,
the answer not, can it be just a quiz?

To all who ask the deep questions of life,

and end up holding the bag from misdeeds now ripe,

with quandary and passion and sincerity cometh,
the merry band which life playeth on it.

The desires and expectations are trampled with the music,
and time rolls on and the opportunity of life loses it.

Quiet and listen for the comforting word,
and take the steps that make a sound that was never heard.

Tread the path of triumph and loss,
the overwhelming sound of the crushing boss,

who lords over one who is ignorant and simple,
the world is that lord rolling over the principle,

of taking for granted life's gifts and promise,
and making a mockery of god's plans, the premise,

that I am one you are and it is an all entwined,
come together in time and space all to ultimately unwind,

as the matrix for all that has become and will be,
when will I ever understand and come this to see.

So I listen and quietly in hopes of destroying,
the pester, the phony, the clown come a peering,

into my world of illusion and sorrow,
revealing the truth of life, in reality the unfettered sparrow.

Glory in the little things

The subtle heartbeat so precious and powerful,
allows me to experience god's glory, a world brimful.

The sound of a bee and the stirring of morning,
call to waking of mind to the infinite forging,

of life on the move, in all directions and methods,
to let me know the grandeur, of life, like strings on levers.

So delicate and mysterious is being and existence,
little is it realized all this happens just for instance.

A miracle, a magical, dance of mirrors,
infinite number of reflections in mind's rivers,

the streams of thought making love to the world,
with the senses touching, the things all a twirl.

Dancing the dance is the touch of the sun,
On my skin are the rays, like children running just for fun.

Where is this place? oh how can I know?,
who cares for this knowledge does it matter is there a foe?

I cherish this place wherever it is,
whether awake or dreaming, I am always a whiz,

at seeing the glory deep down in the center,
at the place where the dancers meet the director,

of life's little glories and sorrows and pleasures,
these and more are life's meaning and measures.

For living and feeling the breezes and noises,
eternal is the magic between time's little poises.

Send me to the place where there is eternal feeling,
In death there not to end, the journey transcending.

For what is there to feel in eternity's bosom,
the laughter of fullness and feeling's fulcrum.

For I am the center, the glory of feeling,
And wherever I may be I am always existing!

The Hell of the Shrewd - The Hell of the Crude

I see hell every day in the eyes of children,
all over the world who have lost their standing in,

societies quest for power and lust,
their eyes have gone cold from the neglect slavery and rust,

of blades and spades thrust deep into their hearts,
by lost souls calling themselves presidents, parents, priests and parts,

of the civilized world which craves for more,
just like the enemy, the terrible infidel of yore.

That enemy over there, the villain, monster and cruel,
if only I had more money to buy more of his fuel,

so I could buy bigger cars and strut my stuff,
and make everyone's life in the world a little more ruff.

Cause I see hell over there but not in my own place,
That would be like saying that my life is but a waste.

For my life is very worthy, happy and true,
No matter that I hate myself, my family and you.

Wait just a minute I did not mean to say,
that life is a boring roll in the hey,

I laugh and smile and agree with what you do,
So long as it helps my cause and no trouble will ensue.

And what trouble can come of my arrogance and disdain,
For the world and all its miracles like life, sunshine and rain,

Which come from the heavens and nurture every vine,

That I use for pleasure, entertainment and wine?

Oh yes the world is wonderful I stay within my walls,
With the television turned up loud so I can hear nobody's calls,

From all those who I have made destitute,
Because of my greed and sanctimonious rectitude.

I am busy running around from morning till late at night,
Keeping the world the way I want it to stay in sight.

For this illusion always serves my purpose,
To pull the wool over the eyes of those who serve us.

And when we have had our fill of the world and its pleasures,
We start a fight so that nobody will see the levers,

For there is no shortage of grievances against our policies,
The way we control other people's lives with controversies.

Those strings attached to everything we do,
That make everyone around us follow our rule.

Conscience be quiet can't you see,
that I am the master and you are a slave to me.

My cleverness has been monumental,
Even in my own household when my family tells me I am mental.

I lord over the world and control all the finances,
And low and behold I do not understand why the flame dances,

As a molotov cocktail burns my house up in a fit of rage,
Because I was never there when my teenager went to a rave.

Now they have all left me, alone and forlorn,
On my deathbed all I bequeath is pettiness and scorn,

I leave vices, bitterness and regrets for posterity,
so that my children will carry on creating more money.

For if my life is worth nothing in virtue,
can't it surely be valued in some sort of revenue?

Is this not the way that I learned while young?
that the meaning of life is measured by a person's corporate rung?

Survival of the fittest is the law of the jungle,
and the world be dammed because I am master of the juggle.

That skillful art of scheme and deception,
Where I tell myself I am the greatest and then you give me an ovation.

I see the hell over there and within me,
This is why I can't bear you to be one with thee.

My toys and gadgets keep me distracted,
To the world we live in which I withheld wealth from, protracted.

Miserable is life, for men, women, girls and boys,
they never promised us a rose garden, just the choice of righteousness or ploys.

And so I'm not so bad after all,
As long as I live as a queen and never bee seen to crawl.

And even as my illusions begin to shatter,
I will build a bigger wall, wave my flag and get fatter.

So that through the fog of my own chronic wheeze,
I will be insulated from all of the desperate pleas.

And this is the hell both at the top and the bottom,
for the haves who have all and the have nots with no forum.

The Next to Last

What is the next to last illusion?
The realization that childhood fantasies are collusion?

How is it possible to reflect on such issues,
when all that is given to the mind leads to tissues,

for the tears of sorrow brought forth by understanding,
that life is at most and at worst no place for grounding.

For cherished beliefs and long held ideas,
are bars for the cell which enslaves the me as,

I go from place to place in the journey of life,
and everywhere become confronted with strife,

of my own making and for my own amusement,
I am always on the lookout for a new recruitment.

With senses bold and desires high,
there is no end in sight, the possibility is never nigh.

And this next to last, it doggedly follows,
the lord of illusions as the heart meekly bellows,

for more of the same, bring it on to the pyre,
like gasoline flames that dance to the fire.

For me there is no illusion but only the written words,
but never did I know they were illusion's serves?

For I knew them through colored eyes,
like the carefree illiterate singing pie in the skies,

singing my own song and tuning the other to the next,
and this is how I created my own web to be vex.

If the illusion was known then why write the letter?
for posterity sake and to hope for merry weather?

This word that is spoken so boldly and true,
reminiscent of childhood's dreams all come ensue.

For how can I know the truth that is spoken to the world,
if there is truth mixed in with cacophony swirl?

The clamor for truth and the uproar of desire,
seem as star-crossed lovers on a voyage set to the lyre.

As they dance to the song of the very same next,
believing they cannot be tainted with the hex,

of truth and lies in the passion of feeling,
as the inner world of faith keeps them reeling.

But the next to last keeps on going, a step ahead,
And never shal they know where to find the snare that has been spread.

Tell them now and tomorrow and in so many imaginative ways,
and yet the grip of the next is the veil that always stays.

For the nest is always boulstered by erudite enjoyments,

as the goal for all life and the purpose of all inducements.

Hail suffering, hail pain, hail dissapointment's bitter sting,
For the only path to be free from the next is frustration's fearsome fling.

That awful dance of victory after the defeat,
of a person's dreams as they fall appart in the heat.

So well and honest was the fight to the last,
only to find that the illusion could never go past,

that threshold of pleasure, the goal of all hype,
where the media tells one can reach the great height.

But the next lives on and the battle always lost,
For hardly there is any who would pay the terrible cost.

Of accepting the truth of illusions to be sought,
the reality that even the teaching is part of the taunt.

For the lords of illusion are not in the world,
they exist in the minds with ideas that unfurl.

So bright and well meaning is to desire to be good,
never for a moment contemplating where the other stood.

Since by necessity and natures unwitting charm,
all have been led to believe they can do no harm.

But to breath and to desire is to cause injury to the sister,
so from the next there is no escape except to life be an arrester,

keeping the illusion from life to dispel,
society's program and the heart's desire to quell.

7

What can be said of the real?
Searching in the world with zeal?

All of my work is done,
And yet never has there been won.

The peace and serenity of time and space,
the longing call in the child's lonely face.

As the serving bowl passes around,
Giving a meager portion without a sound.

What is the real and how is it to be known?
As the constant pursuit is ever again and again sown.

With hazel eyes and chastized pride,
The rebelious nature is sent away to hide.

In places unknown and locales in the sun,
There is always hope for the needy are more and then some.

For passion's pride and struggle's victory,
We make our way believing in history.

And yet we go and then come again,

Still holding dear to the real even when,

The signs are clear and the proof is our sorrow,
that the fights and desires are always hollow.

But yet what is real for the world is hear.
And yet what world it is all so queer.

As the years pass by and the dreams slip away,
We continue to forge and show the young ones the way.

As we learned it from our forebears and all the lives past,
We hold on to the dreams and desires to make them last.

Those dear dreams and desires that drive and compete,
For the attentions of nature to make us complete.

For the real is as the real appears
Never minding the signs and symbols as they whisper in the ears.

Oh no, don't want me I am not sound,
and nowhere in this place can I be found.

Forewarned and forearmed is the motto of the field,

Trace the steps of the journey so the truth may one wield.

For why should it be so that the mind is distracted,
By those transient thoughts that we cling to protracted.

What have they to say for the love of the land.
As they rush in to the mind and blow up a storm of sand.

This storm carries away even the most dedicated aspirant,
like busy destroyers and the most evil tyrant.

And the real is the image that streams through the mind?
Or is it rather the weakness of humanity serving time?

In the wretched condition of time, space and desire's lust,
in these images that pass relentlessly we have learned to put our trust.

And try to stop the river of mind, even for ten seconds,
to discover the woeful weak condition of the intellect's ignorant lessons.

Those long lost years believing in the sights and sounds of life,
Just partaking in the dance of struggle and strife.

And this dance of life where does it end, where does it leave us?
With a mind that cannot hold a single thought, preferring the mischievous.

These thoughts that appear so real and tangible,
Are merely the sights and sounds bombarding the senses so impressible.

The mind and senses so convinced of the reality,
even in dreams do they report on the images as a surety.

In the nervousness of mind and the anxiety of the senses,
there is a magical illusion convincing the eye to let down its defenses.

Caught in the spell, river of movement and desire,
never does the mind want to think of anything higher.

And what is life without the river of thoughts?

Only nothing beyond a thick haze of psychic moss.

Rushing in and rushing out in every moment and every hour,
the mind's eye is always engaged on the lust for experiences and to gain the power.

Over worlds and dreams and desires the ego searches always insatiable,
never stopping, reflecting or longing for that peace that is indestructible.

But when the world no longer satisfies and the heart is disillusioned,
The inevitable question creeps in, what is the real, is it just a profusion?

Of movements and pursuits for desire's insistent sake,
and what meaning have these at the time of the wake?

For all that can be gained and all that can be accomplished,
There is still the burning factor that life has been abolished.

To the earth or to the sea or to the fire it is consigned,
that body that was the venue of the life that was so entwined,

with the pleasures of life that were ever so fleeting,
and for pettiness sake withstood the pain of not succeeding,

in the endless search of fulfillment for life's delights inspired,
to be ever more consigned to the illusion that thoughts conspired,

to keep me going, to the other day and for ever more, if only, just another,
so to speak it is the fate of the terrible one who takes the bother,

of keeping up the fantasy of life as the true and not the game,
for no power on earth can stop the river from believing that there is some gain.

Tell that mind and its river the truth about the image,
only to creep along on fours for the handouts of the parsonage.

Stop the river, dam the dike, discover the eye as witness,
the lonely flight of high flying birds, with vantage beyond illness.

There's the place of nothing taken, nothing gained in the pyre,
And so to become the seer of truth, transcendent worlds to aspire.

So as when the truth of higher worlds becomes the faith of the long-ago,
the empty words of life's rivers and chases become the cosmic embargo.

And never more to allow the intrusion of fate's movements, changing rivers, and fleeting highs,
come to me, if have it all, what you need here if only; all these fall on deaf ears, impotent cries.

For as the nothing enters and the nothing stays so the river moves not and the heart will want not,
therein knowing bolsters, seeing never never lands, like the sunspot, ever burning hot.

Fire fly burns hot, as he strokes the fire light,
fan the flame of heart, blaze away the plight.

Burdensome the world, holding mind in twirl,
hurry away tonight for the wings unfurl.

To the parts unknown, words and thoughts fail to condone,
or to rectify the peace but the illusions are blown.

Truth is not the real, no matter how the senses zeal,
turning world like wheel, no longer having the same feel.

Thus is the real to be known, in time of waking or in dream, when the river reaches the ocean never again to become a stream.

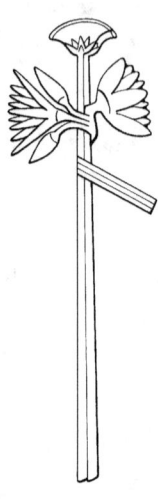

I See

I see the world as it ebbs and flows,
never forgetting what nobody knows,

that time and space are but lingering sparks,
of all the joys and sorrows of the supreme harts.

I move about like leaves in gentle rustle,
by the evening breeze as it blows through leafs without a muscle.

Peacefulness is that drizzle of the morning,
never responsive to the call of warning.

That heed, that caution, the playing with fire,
that play of people with the world leading to mire.

I see and hear and senses are attentive,
yet now and never have to be relentive.

Where I go in this place is no matter the venue,
flow I so like the birds and the bees that are in too,

the world as it is without meaning and purpose,
so long to the desire with intent only to hurt us.

Relaxing on the side found is I in the corner,
Reviewing the landscape like the flowers an adorner.

Where is the better place for being in the journey,
for where we go in past or future is no need for the hurry.

Let I know now for the future is not ever clear,
That knowing is not knowing future but only what is here.

Then is see and I is see for see is I and see is see,
and I am like the ebb and flow, the you and I the river and sea.

Can you feel me now - Part 2

Can you feel me now?
Can you feel me now?

I am hidden in the trees this morning
Even did I give a warning

Shining in the time of dawning
Worlds around for you a calling

See today oh see tomorrow
Clever falcon eyes in sorrow

Forget me not oh can you see me
Together always, hearts a plenty

Can you feel me now?
Can you feel me now?

See me feel me in the meadow
Shining bright my eye upon you

Don't you know there's life for all
Live your life to win or fall

Tell them all about the glory
Today is time, forever glory

Feel me now, I burn, I sparkle
Tonight is love remember and marvel

Fly Again

Don't you want to fly again?
The soul awaits the time to spend.

Such time abides in timeless bliss.
Seems only a lover's passing tryst.

Come back and fly with me again,
And never leave me to the end.

Give yourself to weightless soaring,
Leaving behind the worldly sparring,

of men $ beast who fight in space.
To me come moving with every haste.

Come fly with me to never knowing,
with every glory and every joining.

With me, to me, you and me, like one, two, three.
For I am you and you are me and ever soaring, ever to be.

So long to the ground, we are ever free.
For ever more the seed of the tree.

Come fly again, take off the burden.
The burden is on me, it was never spoken.

Hail all today, to me, and tomorrow,
Fly away from time and space and the sorrow.

The eyes so true, the child and the glory.
When pure flies away, comes the end of story.

Tell them, those fetters, some ideas about the seven,
They are the feeling that arises when flying up to heaven.

Searching all, everywhere, for the taste of the transcendent,
Fly away to the beyond, and from earthliness be ascendant.

What it is – Part 1

Breath in
Clean in

One cannot speak when breathing in
Take care of in, let God take care of the world

Never despise and always realize
The world in time is lost in grime

And I belong in breathe in
Contemplating the lust to always win

Celebrate in breathe in, change up, wake up.

Tolerate, obfuscate, never take the time to wait
on time and goals paying worldly dues and heavy tolls,
in loosing sleep and gods heavenly folds.

Breathe in, world out, live there never despair or doubt.

What it is - Part 2

I am sick and I admit it.
Many times I thought to quit it.

Always spurred and never yearned.
Telling all the subtle world.

You see this and you see that.
Like a scurry mouse after the cat.

So so, now now brown cow,
Never wonder with upraised brow.

Tell me all and tell me true,
So that I may laugh at you.

Talks a lot and in the end saying what?
God abhors the talking a lot.

So and so, too and fro,
Save it all and give no mo.

What it is – Part 3

I am yours and I can't help it.
Servant true and unrepentant.

Though the pace of world incessant,
Carries all to hell in every instant.

There is bliss and there is joy,
In every touch and every ploy.

By the God who pulls the strings,
Of the heart from behind the scenes.

Become one and beckon to all,
To come inside the meditation hall.

To leave the world and the endless swirl,
Like endless top goes on to twirl.

But let me be the child who plays,
And who looks on in varied ways,

From far far away and long long ago,
Right here and right now nowhere to go.

What it is - Part 4

And why do I do it, lost cause the heart does plunder,
No matter how, no cost is enough for the one who knows surrender.

Do it for me or do it for you,
This is the philosophy of one who believes in two.

But I am the one who comes from the one,
And this realization brings so much fun.

For my actions are free of relentless worry,
Even though I sometimes tarry.

All the while I have it all,
Even if I appear to fall.

And action is as action does,
In the beginning how can I say who I was?

So I do it for me and all gods glory,
So as I work the result is already before me.

I have won for I am free,
And what I do never entangles me.

Today, tomorrow is all the same,
As it ever was, revering god's name.

And what I do is nothing to extol,
So long as I continue to play the role.

The Door

The door of peace, it ever bedazzles
The wayward heart beset with hassles

My heart is a pendant
Looking on always observant

At life's little trifles
While they make them their battles

That peace, revered calm
Is the world's most precious charm

To behold and to shudder
Never a word to this world utter

Climb about the wagon train of life
And head for the perilous path of strife

Far away and thought peace is fleeting
It has its own stories and eternal feeling

If I stay this way I can have it all in time
Never mind the world and restless heart inclined

To casting lines for fishing happiness
The family hates after three days of tenderness

I am all content here and alone
This is the reality be it in town, office or on the phone.

So let it be, ad bygones by
No need to say sorry or even explain why

For I know the secret of this place,
It is the riddle of the hearts desireless waste.

Doomed to Silence

Doomed to Silence ever present
Even with knowledge ever crescent.

For who will listen to the swimmer,
Who struggles to move against the river?

And out of time or place belongs
The silver tongue like a lover's songs

Oh heaven awaits and the world repudiates
Clamoring sweet nothings whosoever appreciates

These words abounding out of place or time,
Forevermore seeking the heavenly sign.

To come to hear, to live on to eternity,
Into holiest places but obstructed by the search for prosperity.

Is this the fate, the destiny mediocre,
For those who choose to be green when others are okre?

If so let it be, for the green is the mother,
She let it be far away from the other.

And when the seasons come full circle,
That time and place come calling in the physical.

So the green will be waiting in the horizon
For all who see, donning high minded reason.

Taking Action

Tell me about what you want me to do.
I've wept and pleaded and waited for you

Where is the movement 'twas somehow the promise,
Could those words have been just a beginning, a premise?

To greater thinking and time philosophizing,
About worlds within worlds and how culture could be rising?

Time marches on towards the coming abyss,
And too much talking may lead one to miss,

The point of the talk, those times philosophizing,
Cause its all good as they say, but action is defining.

So words do trap one who takes no action.
Philosophizing about the world and joining a faction.

I believe in this and you believe in that.
Why don't you as a cat what he calls a fact,

About running after mice
Forever will never suffice.

Cause that's his way, today, yesterday and tomorrow.
For that's how he's built and he can never borrow,

The way of the dog or mouse or a man,
As if it could be bottled or processed in a can.

That's him and that's me, a cat of the world.
To cease the movement in a storm awhirl.

Pouncing on the prey after thinking for a while
As the prey mounts up on a rising pile.

Of excrement left due to your inaction,
He leaves a mess forcing your undivided attention.

So the question begs an answer, tell all and share the cat's anger.
Today as yesterday one must become the wrangler,

Of all you survey and all that you see,
Forevermore for all who can be,

The one, the most. The small and the brave,
Do it for them and never misbehave.

So now what? Yes, yes what I hear, hallelujah?
I march on and look back alone cause nowhere were ya.

Never mind my love, I'd do it all again,
For you I breathe and move with paper and pen.
So the story is told evermore for all to gain.

The answer is there

Everywhere written in time and space,
is the ever-present glory, the divine's grace.

Speaking through leaves of a tree or a lion's roar,
The answer always there ever-present, evermore.

To have and to hold is what everybody seeks,
As they pass through life turning pages as weeks.

Of lives that are short or lives that are long,
This is what everyone aspires even as they sing their own song.

As individuals they say this is my life, where I come from who I be,
Yet never understanding all they know is just a creed.

And to say or to believe is not to know or experience,
The glory of the answer, incomparable deliverance.

From all the pains and sorrows of the world,
Begotten as the sails of desire unfurl,

And also from all the joys and losses,
There is no need to bear the humiliation of the crosses.

The answer is there but they cannot see it
Tell them all to go and desire and seek it,

When pursue what you desire
And weep with frustration and ire.

Then the answer comes collective,
All is good and all is connected.

I Belong

I belong to you and all that you are.
I know not the word, it's pain leaves no scar.

I am hopeless before you, my desires waning,
After all those years of fruitless searching.

I tried to have them, the things that catch the eye,
But in the end they reminded me I failed no matter how hard I'd try.

Because from the world and the eye-catching things,
I can count on disappointment at my door when it rings.

Belonging to you, that is all, end of story;
And where are you so I can run in a hurry,

To the things of belonging, the hugging, the cuddling,
In a tree, in a man, in the sky, I adore seeing.

To know you and feel you is always my pleasure.
Forevermore ignorance will never me censure.

Or separate us,
Or loose us,
Or obstruct us!

And this belonging, what can be better if anything can?
The never-ending feeling of being the first fan.

Accepted, forgiven and always smitten,
Through my life, your being, the story is written.

And found am I in you the founder.
I am yours, a servant, a slave and lover.

Beloved in you and in all I bask,
Moving on forevermore fulfilling the task.

Too Much Talking

What is the price of too much talking?
To revel in glee at useless jawing.

Not even gossip is being here referred to.
Rather the needless never new.

There are so many things that need not be said.
In daily conversation why not be silent instead.

All that is needed is acknowledgement on the hearing.
Of what another has said no need for on banter to be leaning.

And so much perception is possible.
For the one who rests in silence more is palpable.

When the mind made restless from too much talking
Is relaxed on the bed of attention and listening,

There is expansion in silence, the art of being quiet,
Even before a word is uttered, the answer is forthcoming, yet,

This knowing the answer without already speaking,
is available when there is not even a whisper.

The secrets of the universe in silence abounds,
For the one who upon listening reflects without making any sounds.

I look around and what do I see?

I look around and see the history,
in every direction abounding volumes.

What do they all say about life?
The pickle it is and all are in?

And who I tell hears but listens not to the words of surrender?

I lose the game and gain the jewel.
As time passes on and I review the drama playing out in life and death.

In the smallest and least things I am free to turn to the one.
So that on one day time will not pass by.

Rather, passing and staying for a while,
As the while is the eternity.

I will love

Love me with all of your being and through this,
Give me whatever it is and I will be with you.

Complete, together, with sun and the heavens I will see.
By day and night for so long and even into old age shall we be.

You will be my friend and mother, lover and salvation.
Take my life, of poor song and play a new selection.

With lips of gold and skin of clouds,
I am your sound.

Nothing here, nor from where I come,
I don't go there,
The pain of life, whole and pure I rely on you.

And there is no other life for me.

Why does it hurt, when closing the green eyes?
Because I cannot see the sun and clouds?

Run, run after life and worldly things
and what is that all about?

Some say it is about nothing,
and others say everything,
and what do I say?

Life hurts much without you.

Therefore, I will love.

I am now

It matters not yesterday, or tomorrow, for I am now.
I slow myself, I stem the tides, and I see the wow,

of eternal moments spreading thin,
into time of life for all to win.

The joy of all the things to come,
in every moment they are the sum,

of glories all a whisper,
for ever an eternal seizer.

I am now and all I see,
Away from all distractions, the worldly sea.

I take my time from moving from here to there,
And thus all I know is there is also here.

For I am now and ever will be,
the fullness of life, contemplating solemnly,

the fullness of time,
when rushing is a crime,

silently the soul house is merely,
the box of life, to get out of wily.

By silence knowing the golden present.
And the next moment like the past, a steady crescent.

Purpose

I move with purpose, purpose I have.
Tell me where you want me to be, to serve or just be the salve.

To go anywhere, to do anything,
To answer the call, to hear the ring.

Your voice is clear,
though far or near.

I long to do the word, the sound.
So I walk the world, the path, I pound.

So more or less.
Or to confess.

The shadow falling,
On life's little calling.

That is my purpose,
in the world, mighty circus.

With mimes and clowns,
In ignorance it surrounds,

The intellect without rhyme or reason,
to confuse and hurt us in each and every season.

For, without purpose we must not be,
or shipwrecked we will become as a boat at sea.

So I move with purpose and I will get through,
to the other side, to be safe with you.

Come to me

Who am I and what do I want?
If I had no thought, no care, no want?

Why does this word persecute me?
Why is it my thought betray me?

Help me oh Divine one, free me!
I beseech you with heart full of sorrows to see.

Oh my child come to me this very day!
I give you nothing, for that is the simplest way.

Freeing up your mind from pouting,
chart a course with voice ever pointing.

Like steps redoubled in pace ever urgent,
to love's embrace, in the eternal void of cosmic regent.

That is me and I am here for you,
just let go of the world and desire filled mind too.

Come to me now in your darkest hour,
I have been here from time immemorial for those who discover the power,

To turn away from the questions and acquisitions,
of mind's agitated with desires and vexations.

For those things mean nothing in the grand scheme.
They are the ego's game, and those playing on its team.

The game is called win and lose and this you must forfeit as player.
Turn in your place to the ignorant player,

who seeks the fulfillment of desire in turn,
and hopelessly goes on, from life to life, suffering, yet never to learn,

the greatest secret of life is not found,
in some thrill or trinket of life which in the world abound.

Come to me and forget all of that,
This is the nothing, the way of enlightenment, this is my pact.

What Sages See

What is the world that sages see?
A place full of people who care only about me?

The sages come from the same place as others.
They experience the pain and sorrow of life and the loss of their mothers.

They sought in vane to fulfill their desires.
Just as worldly people who follow their sires,

Their ancestors who told them of the glories of money,
And meat eating and pleasure seeking, oh to find a honey.

And what sages see in those things is a story,
Of people who have somehow lost their glory.

Forgotten or misunderstood, who they are as if lost in a festive party,
While so many in the world feel the pain of going hungry.

But what can I do? Is the question of many people,
Those others are suffering because their mind is feeble.

This is the answer that the worldly prefer to give,
So they may continue the life they want to live.

Sages cannot live this way because their sight is too deep.
They see the pain and illusion of life, and do not turn away when others weep.

Sages can never seek to live their lives at the expense of others.
So far are they removed from the worldly way of taking care of only one's sisters and brothers.

The world the family to sages,
And all in the world, god's eye, it pleases.

So sages ask how can there be a life for me,
That is separate from all of my family?

How did the world ever come to learn,
To see itself as separate from nature as it does burn?

They pass their lives away as if it were a law,
To indulge in everything they see or saw.

Illusions in life about me and you,
That I can have it all and to hell with those who,

Do not believe as I do because I am right,
I have the power and all the might,
Economic and military so don't bother to fight!

Just jump on the band wagon of lust greed and glut,
It matters not for the world is a rut.

All used and abused by factories busy churning,
The precious objects for profiteering.

Never mind the generations of the future,
Everybody else is just a moocher.

So sages see the play and the plight,
Of the rich and the poor by the day and by night.

The haves and have nots, the ignorant and the media,
Steering the heard to unbounded consumer mania.

And to hate one another for race or creed,
Unlike any other animal on earth to eat and spread seed.

Populations growing out of bounds and in fear,
Of other peoples, religions or politics held dear.

And who is responsible, who gets the blame,
For this situation, is it an achievement or a shame?

The leaders, the chairmen of governments and industry?
Or religions dogmatic who promote orthodoxy?

That ours is the best way the one and only,
And all others are fakeries, the product of speculation and ignorant inquiry?

For we have the answers to all of the questions!
Never mind our culture is broken, full of imperfections.

The drug abuse, and health crisis, the violence in the streets,
Are merely an effect of life as it seeks,

Its balance, its just the economy of supply and demand,
The city is a black hole of loafing people with open hand.

Seeking for handouts because they are lazy and don't want to work,
Never mind that they were taught to be the perfect jerk!

The sages see the fallacy of yore,
The illusions of life, of vanity and more.

For nothing will ever possibly suffice,
When it is pursued with ignorance and vice.

And all is well in heart and mind,
As long as truth is never entertained, any sort or kind.

Because what could be more ignorant and vicious,
Than hoarding wealth, guns and food meticulous,

As others go destitute, embattled and hungry,

As we extol our sacred government, culture and economic philosophy.

The worldly philosophy of owning and controlling,
The concept of superiority, the management of conforming.

Getting fat off the land and the backs of the people,
The slaver and the slave, degrade until unable,

To see the error of the faulted way,
Well what else do sages see, what else could they say?

Sages see the foam and the rubber, the plastic and the glitter,
That fools all the minds who see instead as if it were gold and silver.

The sages see through a purified mind,
Mature and grown up having no need of wine.

No need for fancy clothes,
Or straightened hair or rearranged nose.

The sages see it all,
And knowing all, illusions fall.

So sages are free from pain and frustration,
They avoid the worldly infatuation.

The veil of truth is torn asunder,
And glories untold, they enjoy all the wonder.

How the smiles of those who do not accept others,
Cut later like a knife when the deception one discovers.

Yet like a dog consuming his own vomit,
People go back seeking more opportunities to reach the summit.

With frustrated desire as they continue to learn,
How worldly enjoyments are doomed from beginning they slowly discern.

Overlooking life's lessons is the product,
Of growing up believing in the existence of blind luck.

That life's all chance and subject to fate,
That we must all hold on to our illusions and hate.

Regardless of our failures in relations,
Like so many seekers in so many nations,

Divorce rate is up, and teachers are poor,
Overworked as ever before and we still ask for more?

But believe in us anyway,
We have the training and the right to say,

What is good and what is not,
Whatever your fate is that is your lot.

In ever more slick ways let us extol,
So that we may build just another mall.

Ok yes we have problems but doesn't everyone?
But we have the mot of all and we have all the fun.

So give up trying,
And start your crying.

For all hope is lost for all you foreigners,
If you are one of those not ruled by our governments and proxy leaders.

What do sages see in this?
Escapism, illusion and certainly not bliss!

For true happiness cannot be found,
in running after worldly goods or illusions of grandeur confound.

Happiness is freedom from illusions,
Covetousness, mental anguish and all confusions.

The list of life's follies could go on and on,
One after the other without indication,

Of where the end is to be found,
Going hither and thither searching in circles round and round.

No solution will ever be discovered,
Until the illusions of life are one's business to be uncovered.

Sages see a world of trouble,

They also see the way to what is noble.

Partaking in cosmic glories,
While sidestepping life's stories.

Sages see so much potential in people,
To elevate themselves not by platitudes, dogmas and steeple.

But by humility, meditation, service to humanity and support of the enlightened master,
For they are the holders of the keys to the gates of ancient lore and the power to muster,

True answers for life's inconsistencies,
How to become the master of fantasies.

How to discover the true meaning of life,
How to cleanse the heart and end all strife.

Where is true happiness ever to be found,
In words of sages and obedience of followers rings the sound.

So set your heart to see what sages see,
The first step is to face the foolish me.

Then take quick steps,
Redouble them and have no regrets.

For at the end of the journey of life all your objects are left behind,
At the end of the quest for glory you take with you what ever you find.

For expansion in consciousness is not like objects,
It can't be taken away, like a car or a case of novelettes,
Let it all go, and seek for true experience,
Of life purpose, its meaning with all due diligence.

Days

It takes days, rolling into weeks and then months to get to the real.

Why don't you stay with me?
Play it for me.

See me through to the end.

Its so hard to be real,
Hard to do the real.

And so I am here for days,
working towards the real.

Tell me about your real.
Do you have a real deal?

to work for in your life?
or is there nothing but foolish strife?

Mine is the bomb, the electric!
The eclectic soul of it all!

And for the days and weeks and months,

The picture comes together and I see the real.
It is my real deal.
Upon which I live and breathe and even utter a squeal.
Oh, I squeal about life and this and that, for I am real.

And so I shout all about.

For all the days and weeks and months and forever more.

The Storm - 2

Watching the waves
      they rise and fall.

Tomorrows pain
      the next day's call.

And to what for I listen,
      the dew as it glistens.

The beauty of creation,
      to me an invitation,

to listen and tarry,
      know no worry, no glory.

The storm of the fire,
      in mind's eye desire,

and the goddess comes,
      to extinguish the fire,

'twas started by malcontent,
      frustrated desire.

I wait and I watch,
      malcontent for abating.

Let the waves raging harsh,
      turn to silk scintillating.

To kindle the dreams,
      of the purest thinker,

for those who mean to
      let her come hither.

She takes me to arms,

so golden and warm.

Protecting me from all harms,
    the body so warn.

Her wisdom stops the torment
    of life led discontent.

To bitter sweet realization,
    of life's exaltation.

Oh say it is something,
    what she has done through speaking.

Can't say it is nothing,
    for me it is cutting.

Away with the evil,
    of foolish desires.

Grow up and realize,
    it is always my time to lead you from the mire.

I too cry dear child,
    for so long you have suffered.

And from time immemorial have I called
    as you muttered.

Between the grumblings of your heart,
    the words never arrived.

Like a boat endlessly wandering,
    on rough seas with pride overflowing.

And now you understand that
    peace is not found in deliverance but in acceptance.

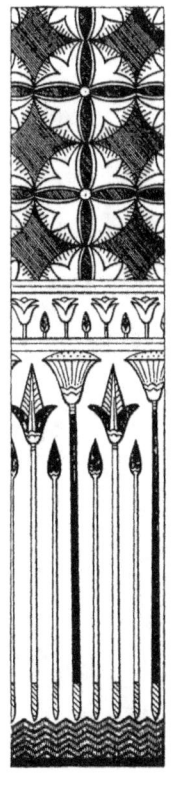

Dear child never want,
       never desire,
              never expect.

And never worry about the storm of discontent.

Freedom

How was I freed?
I understood and I let go.

Letting go of what?
The burden of desire.

Desire to do what?
Desire to achieve.

What was there to achieve?
Whatever mind fancied to have.

What was the fancy of the mind?
Believing the way that things are supposed to be.

Where did you learn about believing in some way that things are supposed to be?

From mom and dad and friend and foe and from TV and school, presidents, priests and you and me.

I once believed in the things of the world,
       the values and the pleasures and having it my way.

But what set you straight?
The wisdom from suffering.

How did you suffer?
I achieved, I pursued, I acquired all I wanted but fulfillment and peace and contentment eluded me.

So what did you do then?
I understood and I let go.

Understood and let go of what?

I understood I gain nothing from all I have without fulfillment and peace and contentment so I let go of all I acquired or will get in the future.

And this is the key?
The key to freedom.

And what is freedom?
Freedom is not being burdened by having or not having,
    but most of all,
        freedom is immunity from the inner voice of discontent.

What is the inner voice of discontent?
The inner voice of discontent is the torment of unrest whose cause is association with and faith in the world.

But without association with the world what else is there?
Association with other.

Other what?
I cannot define it but it is freedom and glory and peace and bliss and openness.

Openness to what?
Openness to reason.

Why is reason so important?
Reason so important because ignorance clouds the mind and then I become discontent.

When I am clouded I forget I am all, I have all I am full and complete.

Reason is the key to understanding and letting go unburdens the mind from the pressure of egoism.

So reason and letting go lead to freedom?
Indeed, reason and letting go lead to freedom.

Distortion

Its funny, watching the mind,
when distortion make it swirl and wind.

Around the inner recesses of the heart,
the heat of desire spreading apart.

Charging around, the sentiments loosened.
Thoughts are clouded by ego they are burdened.

Distorted thoughts, stirred up and swelling,
The mind sees through murky feeling.

And reason fades away to where?
Away, fallen prey, to desire's spear.

Waiting, watching, understanding abated,
The long lost trail of life un-syncopated.

The path of balance beckons the calling,
ever present whirls of eternity are looming.

Order and peace are the answers to ills a plenty.
Reality and contentment are the cure to the many,

Many thoughts and disparaging ideas,
are forgotten at the time of joy beyond tears.

This is the time of love everlasting,
when truth is revealed and the mind is for taming.

The Wise Man

I play the role of wise man but what do you know of me?
The words are said and the clouds ahead but what do you really see?

The person with garb, the personality with teaching
And time is fleeting so long to the weeping?

Is this what you think of me so distant and cloudy?
Ever missing the essence and all the true glory.

For what am I but reflection of singing?
That song of the soul that longs to hear spirit calling.

But to your eyes the wise man,
To your eyes the holy man

And this eyes past the plan
Of forbidden farmers crop

That planting bringing sorrow melting,
Bitter harvest, that of not relenting.

Ever forceful ever desirous
Going away from me seeking the unrighteous

Forget the wise man he's just an illusion
Take the I man, take the I woman infusion.

Believe in me not and eyes will be pleased immensely
Tomorrow's walk will be reward for thee.

Seek the wise man listen listening and forsake the man
For the role is merely a play, a slight of hand.

Build the body of light a do like the sage in ever age.
Play the role and step to the crumbly stage.

Join the wise man, play with the nice man of this world.
So the world will not win and send you into a mental twirl.

Hay, the high and mighty, the righteous ones hear the wise man.

All I have to do

many years ago you asked me,
what do I have to do to be with you?

And I said:

> Rest with me,
> be with me,
> talk with me.

but you moved to the world and tried to shape it
with toil and blood you may yet do it.
But no matter your success is it really worth it?

Let me take care of those who can't.
And I am still here saying rest and be and talk.
That is all there is to do, right here and there.

Be with me and we will spend eternity.
Be with me and experience the glory.

Nothing matters in me, and matters all are in me.
So be with me and all matters are fulfilled.

Breathe me, see me, always be with me,
I will never leave and never deceive thee,
No matter where the ever be.

You know the way
In the early morning when the world is asleep,
Be awake to the eye that is buried deep,

Within, behind the mind,
and there you will always find,

Oh me and thee!
And forever never leave me.

Time, time and away and afar,
Forget the roads and deeds and goal of old souls.

Renew yourself in the waters of plenty,
To discover the greatest high within me.

Be with me… Be with me… Be with me…

Glory of Glories

Gory of Glories I was told,
To be in the zone, the place of old.

Never a whisper, neither a whisper,
The place where nothing grows, only for the listener
 of infinite glory and magnanimity.

Lucid charms of spiritual synchronicity.
Beyond all time and space I gather my members of mind, the end
of chatter.

Close the door on words and actions,
Always the clamoring worldly reactions.

That place opens up for the clean and pure,
Who desire to reverse from more to fewer.

To touch or to see the glory of spirit,
To lose oneself beyond boundless limit.

The journey of life has meaning after all,
Even after the painful ego falls.

There it leaves you blind and forsaken,
But never are you abandoned by souls words which hearken,

Truly there is no way to describe,
The realm of the transcendent, even for a skillful scribe.

It must be experienced in fullness and peace,
The juvenile movement of worldly release.

    From low to high
    From pettiness to magnanimity
    From small to all
    From negative to positive

The road bends and nerves are frayed,
But in the end God is never delayed.

For she is in me and in all things,
Waiting for my mind and love to take wings.

To fly up to the transcendental regions of light,
To catch the glory of spirit in mortal sight.

Oh lady of glories awaken your fierce nature.

I await you eagerly.
I await your presence.

I offer this child as the canvas of your work.

May you mold and burn this aggregate of elements.

May you have your way as an insistent mother who is caring and wise.

Cause the pain and consume the darkness.

Carry me to the height of heights, on the journey of journeys.

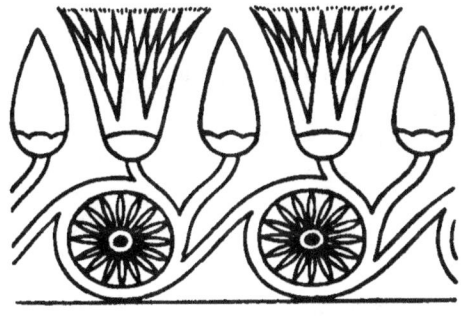

If there was no trouble

If there was no trouble in the world,
What would be there to set you in a whirl?

Who would turn you out?
Who would send you out?

Of you complacency and desire,
The long time unquenchable fire,

Of lust for things,
As if they had wings.

Upon which pleasure floats up higher, and higher,
As if true and abiding happiness they could inspire.

Tell me the answer to this riddle.
The plenty that always leads to the little.

Nay, refuse for the answer is in your face,
Tiredness and frustration with the fruitless race.

The youthful years spent in getting it all,
To find it all ends in a selfish brawl.

With yourself or with relatives,
or with whoever fancies your imperatives.

So let the trouble send you,
let it break and mend you,

don't turn around
and mess around,
with kiss and making up
and suffer and put up

don't go back around,

to the last round,
and find in the end
a punch drunk friend

of the world who beats you,
maligns and mistreats you.

Turn away and use it,
The use and abuse from each hit,

Of the world, turn away and make a place,
Apart from the hectic race.

Of running hither and thither,
So far from the hidden master.

Who leads away from all sorrows,
That the world, from it the ignorant borrows.

Let the world push you,
To seek the peace of the special few.

Who find a way to freedom,
Away from the illusion of egoism.

Don't bother with telling the world come on is that all you got?
Never mind, just realize that what appears real, really is not!

And when this realization truly dawns,
The search for truth leads away from the one who mourns.

Cries of loss and pain and the trouble of life,
Then the search for enlightenment becomes the good vice.

And this desire is the greatest egoism,
Which opens up the inner prism
Of the seven gateways that lead up to heaven.

That Place

That place where darkness falls,
I knew this place so far beyond the walls,

So long ago so far in time,
There was a place no thoughts entwine,

For therein lie the greatest ties,
that bind us all and no human cries.

Oh darkness fall and there is nothing there,
No life or death, now all is clear.

Take it back, take it all the way,
To that place where one cannot hear them say.

You lose or will, no meaning is binding,
Lords place, timeless worlds abounding.

Knowing nothing and seeing infinity,
In that place which is neither here nor there completely.

Within, deep down it is for the keeping,
Today, yesterday and tomorrow always heaping.

Peace eternal is the here and now,
Through the milk, oh Lord, of the Golden Cow.

To that very place straightaway take me,
That place oh lord where you greet me.

How can I keep on roughing in this,
Or that the place could ever escape and miss,

the all, the time, the peace Divine.
May it find me, that dark place, where no thing I can ever find.

Sanctuary

In that special place,
I went within and saw the face,

of my beloved, dear, so long awaited.
Never forsaken or glory abated.

Available in the deepest, longest, widest expanses,
But accessible only through the briefest glances.

Burning up the memories of impotence,
Sailing along without slightest consequence,

To see the beginning and ending of all things,
The heavenly song and bell that rings,

For all who come to the special place,
Leaving behind all mortal trace,

To discover what and who and who and what,
It is all about and all a part.

Let me go there again and again!
So long to the world of illusory friends.

The clouds of desire,
Fall on funeral pyre,

and taking flight with the wings of gold,
I become the myth and stories that were ever told.

I Am Universe

I am universe, space abounding.
Fires & maelstroms all surrounding.

Taking all within my mind,
I go within and turn in kind.

To all that space filled with planets and moons,
Emanating cosmic chants and tunes.

Extolling the glories that I am,
And all universe contained within me as a clam.

And even more am I so vast and occult,
That space of darkness wherein I summersault,

in dance and gayety, laughter joyous,
I look on to see for all of the pious.

Who worship me as nature, stars or idols,
Wherever they go there I am, always idle.

Seeing me wherever they go, I escape through blinded longing,
Hiding there and everywhere, leaving all to do their pining.

For what they think of me I cannot say,
Tomorrow, yesterday or never, searching for the way,

Of light and life, oh precious game.
That causes all to miss the glory of my ever-present fame.

For I am the universe and all that is in it.
Hate me, love me, care not, no matter, never mind, forget it.

For I am universe, the all, the everything,
Whatever they do it matters not, for I am the object of their seeking.

I know

To you I say I know.
All the things that people sow.

The triumphs & failures, joys and sorrows,
All this comes when a form from nature one borrows.

Time & bodies to pursue the things for clinging,
Never mind the search for a real meaning.

"I know" is said by most people, most often,
By those who feel secure in the dreams that soften.

For those which the minds and hearts willing to be seekers,
Of transcendental truths to be the revealers.

Others have little lives and petty things to follow,
Doomed are they to an existence of limitless sorrow.

I know what this is, after all it was once my life.
Taking from the world & receiving gilded strife.

I know the glory of peace everlasting,
Subtle worlds, with light scintillating.

Through purple flames and hazy schemes as crucible,
I have no mart in it anymore, the world you see, is inscrutable.

Knowing knows no way of ignorance,
Buried flames of desire dismissed through learned experience.

Seductive, capricious, worrisome memories and images,
Are nothing, of no concern to the fearless enlightened sages.
Know this and live, love and master,
Worlds within worlds, averting every disaster!

I knew my heart

I knew my heart,
I played the part.

Then came the time,
I lost all sense of rhyme.

I thought could never survive,
The anguish of loss of what makes me live.

What I knew I struggled to see in life.
What I'd do became a way of strife.

I knew my heart,
I played the part.

I knew the way to paradise,
Turning away from compromise.

Looking away to feelings that stray,
Forgetting the path, the singular way.

Sending the world my deepest feeling,
Sensing that time was ever fleeting.

I knew my heart,
I played the part.

I stop, and look at my heart,
Oh tell me, I already know, I need a new start.

I see a golden line,
Pounding the mind in time.

Leading the way to heaven,
Singing the song to hasten,

My way back to you,
Calling me back to you.

I knew my heart again,
I never lost my best friend.

I knew my heart,
I played the part.

Neter is we

I used to say there is nothing hither.
But one day I discovered the Neter.

So many times I spent longing for higher love.
So I searched high up in the clouds above.

Glowing crimson golden sandalwood,
expresses the aroma of heaven where I stood.

When Neter came to me and told me,
The glories of life and the magic of the three.

Time and time again gloried.
Words and sights of cosmic time a carried.

Filled me lifted me left me,
away and afar, no matter, all was always three.

Everywhere I saw the three,
How could it otherwise be?

Now I am blinded for life you see.
Because I no longer see you or me.

Or Divinity exalted, family to be lauded.
Nothing polluted, nothing diluted.

All I see is the golden three,
rapt up in what was once me, thee and we.

So I am one in three,
Do you also see what I see?

Neter told me so in trance,
even though I knew in advance.

Reading all the works of old,
let me know the philosophy that was told.

Long ago and far away in time.
Never mind the wisdom mine.

Yet I never truly knew,
until the faculty of sight I withdrew.

Oh Neter, O glory,
Tell me more and fill me with your story.

Tell me how it all began.
How the world and endless universe did stand.

Or better yet bring me understanding,
so that I may whisk away to transcending.

And Neter granted me understanding and story,
for there and then the answer was clearly.

Understanding and transcending are two sided of truth.
As much as the spirit goes up through the roof.

When vision and understanding are ripe in the mind,
they move the seer to heights leaving the world behind.

And when I leave the world behind forsaken,
no more me is to betaken.

And therefore there is no three.
Me and you and universe are Neter, Neter is wee!

Original Wisdom

Original wisdom is the thing you know.
You know and yet another road you sow.

Disregarding the truth that is understood even,
When the road desired is ominous and unproven.

On that path the energy and wits are frayed,
Because due to lack of foresight, mind by ego is swayed.

The original thought is often right.
So one should forget the second thought that comes into sight.

Just clear the mind and listen closely,
To the inner self, to listen silently.

For the voice of reason is calm and clear,
To desire, fear and doubt never lend and ear.

Original wisdom saves all from trouble,
With mistakes abounding life will crumble.

The art of life is clouded and dark,
Come here or go there, always missing the mark.

To err is human to forgive is Divine,
But to ignore the voice within is worse than a crime.

Take away the pettiness and sloth of life.
Repulse them always with peace and working for the without strife.

Strifeless work that is free of desire,
Is that divine work that has a special fire.

The fire that burns away despair and disappointment,

For lack of worldly desire promotes no enrollment,

In the ranks of people who fight every day,
Forgetting what is right and going after what they want any which way.

So work rightly and remain at peace.
Do this by keeping the balance, never pursue this tirelessly and never cease.

Offer your actions to God the most high,
And enjoy contentment, and to heaven draw nigh.

Don't fool yourself, settling for second best,
Thinking "this is sufficient, this will do, forget the rest."

Forgetting your potential is forgetting yourself,
And settling for second best is poverty regardless of your wealth.

Money can buy you a thin,
But nothing makes the here to sing,

Like precious moments in contemplation,
Of freedom ringing with no anticipation.

Original wisdom is what to live by,
Thoughts and actions that never lead to sigh.

Filling the heart with the teachings of heaven,
I never need to think again, to ask the brethren.

For original wisdom is what I knew,
But forgot when busy life did ensue.

So now is take the time to listen,
To the whispers of innermost inspired rhythm.

That cosmic music that harmonizes and organizes,
And makes all to have a place, all kinds and all sizes.

Original wisdom is that which I will know,
And no way again to ignorance saw hello.

Original wisdom is all I need,
And every act in life will be its seed.

And with that seed I shall grow a tree,
A tree of life and a tree of glee.

With original wisdom I shall always be bountiful,
With inspiration and wisdom always plentiful.

Original wisdom is who I am,
That ignorance and quandary is just a scam.
Original wisdom is what you are reading,
Can you follow its ancient teaching?

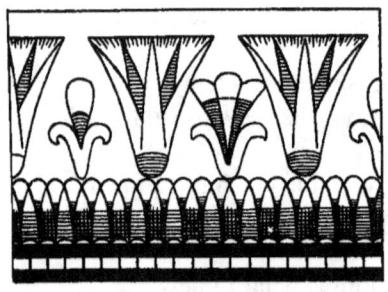

I am sick

I am sick and what does this mean?
Do I lament, who is me, do I become mean?

Do I hate the god of life and death?
Do I lament over things that I once left?

I am down and low.
I am tortured and why so?

Nobody knows yet everybody knows.
While in bed, body immobile, I ponder over woes.

In this condition I see my life and word and deed.
The things of the world that I want and yet do not need.

For I have come to see that all is passing,
And I am realizing, body made of not for lasting.

And all that remains is that eternal sun.
The force that causes all to run.

The sun, golden divinity of perfection and glory.
Discovery that I am the beginning of that study.

Not the body nor the thought, nor the desire am I.
Tortured or pleasured neither weathered to a sigh.

No need to frown, pain reminds me of the one.
That beauty of release, eternal peace.
Burning to ashes, loving rays through time and space.

Wings

Flying on wings of wisdom's song,
To ever walk on breezes,

Tenderly feeling, gingerly gleaming,
Eyes of wondrous splendor.

Curves of cosmic spheres aloft,
Coming down and never lost.

To me and all to see for one,
Forever more and eternity.

I am there telling the tale of wondrous glory.
For I fly along on wings of golden eyes and crimson colored
wings of endless story.

Rain & Rays

I love the rainy days,
And purple rings of golden rays.

Rain can stop the play and plans,
The desires that were in mind during weekly caravans.

To work and back,
And to and fro to school you know.

But rainy days are so much more,
To go within and see what is in store.

To stop and think and hear the sound,
Steady pounding on heavenly ground.

Caring soul asks "tell me all about the stress?
The sorrow, the problems that seem endless.

Stopping, rainy days make me look within,
And say, "I remember that the soul's the God in touch with them.

They who are the source of life's desire,
They breathe the love that fuels the fire,

In me to live and breath on sunny and rainy days.
Since the beginning of time and in all ways.

Through rain I know of darkness and grayness,
And in sun I know the life of water's coolness.

But rainy days are more tell me more,
Those days are closer to the eternal darkness of ancient lore.

For I am light and life abounding inside,
Like a shining sun that cannot hide.

Yet I am darkness that knows the inner being,
Who lights up all with just a glimpse seeing.

Opening the eye I shine on all,
And from my place of darkness I am the source of all.

Those rainy days remind me of my eternal waters,
The ultimate reality beyond the borders,

Of conscious thoughts and desires,
Borne of worldly musing that never tires.

I am more than these,
And to rainy days and solar rays I for this thank and say "more please!"

The Silent Times

The silent times with you my soul,
I treasure more and more over time as they unfold.

To pass and hold the time aloft,
The gleaming hue so light and soft.

It is like no other time when body is sound.
When television's voices and mischievousness is off.

Companion Divine, communicating without talk,
To have and hold this time alone with you,
Is greater is greater than speaking to millions.

Oh in the silent times with you I feel eternal!
Crying tears of joy like pearls of dewy light I do declare.

Those silent times are no longer rare.
Holding me and I hold you.
Together always as if I always knew.

And time matters not, nor do the words or sights.
The time in silence, beyond time itself,
Piercing all and what else!

The silent time was nothing like it,
Forsaking all else and turning to it.

This is the path to soul and life eternal.
Well so long to words.
Hello to more of silent times with you my love.

Flying High

Flying high above the clouds,
In glowing bodies, leaps and bounds.

Going up in the jet I gaze at the heavens,
All around me I see the products of the senses,

The people, the desires, the plastic, the metal,
And where is the peace of the lofty vessel?

The mechanical bird is certainly a marvel.
But there is no substitute for flying high on the wings of goddess's glory.

Being carried and nurtured like the child in the story,
Purified by wisdom and infinite love surely.

For these are the wings that raise up the mummy.

And I am so high far beyond the earth bounds,
That everything I see below is like a speck, all sights and sounds.

Together as one everything devoid of individuality.
And this is the far and away ultimate reality.

So ask me not to come down to the level,
Of being below with the ignorant rabble.

Let there be light far above and below.
Let there be sight and hearing of the teaching so,

There will be goodness down there for thee and for all,
And may ignorance wane, may lust, jealousy, and greed we forestall.

For I want that place, away from perdition.
May all of god's glories ever come to fruition.

And may I be there in the place of transcending,
Beyond life's little challenges, the struggles be ending.

Anger

Tell me why instead of a sigh,
Instead of a frown, instead of a lie,

I find myself making use of anger,
Not a friend or neither a stranger.

All of the years of working to foster,
Personality pure, brimming with luster.

Nevertheless the power comes forming,
Destroying what is in the path, all-consuming.

Can it be there is remnant of feeling,
The kind that lies deep in believing,

That losing and gaining are real and abiding?
Can it be still a lack of awakening?

The dawning has come and the light grows steadily.
Yet in the mind remain lurking most evilly,

Thoughts that linger, impure and restless,
Due to the lack of intellect as witness.

Unhurried thinking that leads to charity.
The kind that leads to truth and freedom from quandary.

Based on original wisdom, the answer of the beginning,
Before it was tainted by too much talking.

Old friend and stranger is still needed and effective,
To emanate the vestige of unwise reflective.

Any way just take heart and know that,
Observe this and see about what,

The glory of the goddess,
The destroyer brings to the overall process.

And let me forget the world

So many things I have done,
And most was not for fun.

Chasing dreams over land and seas.
Never mindful of what soul sees.

Watching, hearing, smelling, touching.
Tasting dishes that are for mass appealing.

Nowhere to run and nowhere to hide,
And taking life along in stride.

And life ebbs and flows to end of days.
My mind's regrets and things undone for time not stays.

Marching on and on as clouds roll on blue skies above,
Taking on scintillating forms I've learned to love.

The Riddle of Life and Free-Will

The riddle of life is the things we see and do and hear, what we follow, what we desire, what we believe in. Where to go? What to do? Why? and When? These are the means- to life as it is known or life beyond- this is free will. The teaching is a road, less traveled and for the strong, like pregnancy it is a road taken categorically. Of three the call was one. Not a demand but and ancient admonishment; Not an order but a guideline, a roadmap of the prescribed sagely way -yet in decrement. One being unfeasible where is victory in the mysteries?, elevating the convict?, achieving Degrees? or each one teach one? Best then to pause, reflect, studying will. Until the time is found, and the Hawk's eye is set and obstacles are like oceans of dreams that dry up in the scorching mist of dessert storms and the lady comes with wisdom aplenty, calming, soothing, loving, putting together what could not be done before; and the end of all ends is nigh.

What I love

What I love is the morning dew,
Streams of golden glistening streams I knew.

The trail that follows the quest inspired.
So far away and yet has sired

Hastened steps to seek and discover,
Morning glow, feeling of a joyous lover.

Embracing blue skies and green meadows,
Cotton fields and blooming fellows,

Those who blossom, seeing life unfold,
In every rain drop, contemplation is the mold.

For appreciating the grandeur of created things,
And the magic of how a bird flies and sings.

Praises, to cosmic being who manifests in colors,
Of all we see and also the unseen others.

I love the air, clarity purity of mind,
Void of space the ocean divine.

Those changing seasons with rustling leaves,
Changing color with coolest breeze.

The quiet Sunday morning,
Or even in the middle of a crowd roaring.

Wherever I go in people or in storm,
This vision will never leave me forlorn.

That I carry in me the seed of light,
Which makes me divine, I am full of might.

I love being, just being, existing and experiencing,

For this, body or not there is always pleasing.

That is what I love.

And what of slime,
And salty summer brine?

The foul smells of excrement,
The thawing plans that is ever-present.

The things that are desired that can never be fulfilled.
All that is wanted, all that is willed.

That is the pain of life,
The eternal strife.

And these things are hated,
And yet desire is never abated.

Well the sages say both the things that are loved and the things that are hated,
Must be left behind if enlightenment is anticipated.

So I say to those things I love and I hate,
Never wonder and I will never wait.

For I am away from things evanescent,
For I am all that is ever present.

Yea I am the one who will never worry,
For I am the guardian of ancient glory.

So the sages say to never care,
For things that loom and then are not there.

And I listen to the call of the wise and the free,
For evermore like on to them, soaring aloft in starry space will I be.

And let me forget the world (Part 2)

Oh tell me something true about the world,
Torn apart mind wanders all a whirl.

Let me be free to be, let me be free,
To see undying days of boundless glee.

Where mysteries and cries of wretched souls not are burdened.
As I realized the way so all of a sudden.

Here I see a way to freedom.
Solemn oath to follow reason.

There oh there I know not living.
I breathe the air without conceiving.

Lost the world, forgotten in time.
I go about ever avoiding a crime.

Remembering the world, it traps, the wings cannot unfurl.
So set me free, oh let me forget the world.

Bathing

So good is the scent of clean,
Breathing air as fresh as a country scene.

Greenery and sunlight, pearls of wonder,
Glory of this world, sun shines down under.

Easy steps, no pain no worry,
Nevertheless not the end of story.

Time marches on, for how long none can say,
But all struggle along to find their own way.

To peace and blessedness, the time of truth,
Clearing away the ego's fruit.

Bathing the body, trim and lean,
Prepared for the journey to where may seem,

To be the ultimate joy and peace aplenty,
Bathing again for truth being ready.

Cleansing bells and stolid wells,
And dreams of old that desire sells.

All fate is washed and lumbering steps
Give way to alacrity and sun never sets.

On purity's brow, the seat of the serpent fire,
Who plays the role of mover and sire.

Oh cleanse the body and mind where soul evolves,
And see the glory of what wisdom tells,

That all is one and one is all.
It was thus in the beginning and even after the fall.

That cleansing and bathing nullified ego torn asunder,
To open the heart and enable it yonder…

all the things

and all the things that we can do,
flying high in the sky and to the depths ensue.

Technology springs from the mind in time,
But not considering the price of wine.

So drunk is the mind in dazzling lights
Mesmerized by the dancer in sparkling tights.

The tall buildings and fast cars look so very good,
The price to pay in time who would?

The one who desires therein lies the dazzle,
That makes them run after things even to a frazzle.

Everywhere it is all the same,
Whether traveling in , America or Africa or Spain.

So all the things they are the same all around,
Even as them may appear different all abound.

With illusory temptations that lead to confusion,
Sending hearts a flutter, with apparent profusion.

For they are all made up of the same elements, the same matter,
So tell the heart never mind forget the pitter patter.

And let it rest, let it find its calm.
Let it feel the gentle soothing balm,

Of peace that is transcendental, the peace that is eternal,
The peace of the supreme, the most high potential.

Secret of the Blue Lotus

Down under I am deep in the soil at the bottom of the pond.
Rising up through the murky waters as I stretch my slender wand.

From darkness and mud I move and dampness I rise,
Piercing through veils of glassy illusion the surface gives way to the sun, grand in size.

Higher still I rise up beyond,
The wetness to breathe the air and I am fixed on.

Golden rays that melt the heart,
Beckoning me to make a start.

Alas he calls me I hear the beacon,
Shining brightly, the one without a second.

Spreading wide my blueness to greet thee,
Give of all come and touch all pass through me.

A thousand times of days and nights,
I rise up and close up responding to the lights.

Golden rays of loving touches,
Lights up my thoughts like little torches.

At night I turn away and look within,
Never a way to darkness give in.

I take the light that was given to me,
And rejoice inside and build on to see

Beyond the world with its many things,
I am free, far from their shadowy stings.

That haunt the mind and make it desire,
For more to feel and lust inspire.

My love and thousand pedaled fire,
Is devoted to the one who is my sire.

The golden one who is blue within,
That is my very self I see in him.

And as I wake for another day,
I let to morrow be as the sages say.

For those who turn away from darkness and choose the light,
Will always have clear vision that coveted spiritual insight.

So breathe in the lotus and drink is fire,
The fire of the sun from whence all is higher.

Expanded heart and loin for birthing,
Growing consciousness, ignorance lessening.

Oh blue one, since the time of Asar,
Tell me your secrets and never be afar,

Intoxicating fragrance, transcendental journey,
Inspired waters, oceans aplenty,

So I sail on lotus water-resistant petals,
Crossing over oceans of dreams and never carrying morals,

Of worldly values and desires and feelings,
The ever-present pressure to actions seedings.

So I am lotus, blue and free,
Always remembering the sun is me.

I am lotus solar and abundant,
Thousand petalled blooming ascendant.

Blueness takes me to glories utmost abode,
I am lotus, blue from the beginning of time and this is my eternal ode.

On Suffering

"To suffer, is a necessity entailed upon your nature, would you prefer that miracles should protect you from its lessons or shalt you repine, because it happened unto you, when lo it happened unto all? Suffering is the golden cross upon which the rose of the Soul unfolds."

If it can be said that the sojourn of life is difficult or a toil it is truly so and it is also not. What is suffering? For indeed where would we be without suffering, to make us stronger, cleanse our souls, or free the mind from illusions and longings? And so how could something that does all this be considered an infliction; only those who do not foresee view it thus. Everyone suffers the pain of life but those who would be wise accept this and use it to their everlasting advantage. As austerity looms so too the freedom shines forth, and as toil produces blood, sweat and tears, it brings forth foundations, pillars and many layered tiers, one above the next, as a ladder to heaven. So who has suffered, who has seen the difficulty, who has lost and what is there to lose? Well in truth if you seek foresight you will find it in the past, in letters written before the journey came to pass. Reading closely all you will find, that the move's unfoldment in time's passing were laid bare, how it would unwind. Nevertheless purity is always the goal. And without sacrifice there can be no evolution of the soul. So opportunities come and go in life. Together with ease, sometimes pain but also with strife. And if he question is being asked this is the time to reflect on life's twists and turns. What does this mean what happened here, what a person understands and learns. From this situation there is clarity for all who seek. Search for meaning and this movement leaves one strong and not weak. Temptation is to see the road as low or high. Forgetting that the higher power governs all from on high. Yet the power wielded never favors the seated. So movements in action can never be depleted. On the path to enlightenment sacrifice is the key. What one does for all, that to is for we. So the answers are clear for an attentive seer. There is no escape for the far or the nearer. Nearer to the field of action the plane of the living, the world of time and space. That is except for those who have transcended, those who have traveled yonder, those who have seen the throne and taken their place. Would that there would be no questions. Would that there would be no lies. Then there would be no reflections; then there would be no replies. From sages, and wise ones the world would be a stranger. It would be worse than now for at least now the world perceives a danger. Because voices of love sing sweetly and softly. Praising the potential and cautioning the folly. That is life and death and all the world's feeling. This should be enough to send a thinking person a reeling. And yet somehow that same ideal, the highest goal, the supreme abode, the sweetness of life eternal, has been colloquially relegated to life's sequential ups and downs and twists and turns. And thereby, thinking in that way a person never learns. The world is so, the world is suffering and toil. And yet all will turn out in the end and there is no reason to boil. But yet the world is a moving, a whirling ball of mud in space and the ocean of infinity. And there must be movement to come to the end of incarnating insanity. Despite your duties, work and family, there must be time allotted for prayer and homily. If this is what you want, what it is, then that you get. Never mind to ask a question about life's little mysteries, just say let it be and don't' regret. Let it be, I am you and you are thee. There is no more to say and neither is there more to see. For what more there is to see and hear requires the care and sense to fear. Not people, not time, not sacrifice which are ensuing, but the loss of soul, the degradation of ignorance, the lack of self-knowledge in worldly pursuing. For if there is any toil it is for the sake of those who seek. If there is any sacrifice it is done for those who are meek. If there is any time it is for those who know what they want, what there is to want, to the world, move they shant. To the teaching, headlong and double stepping, eagle spreading, never relenting, steps of gold higher and higher they go beyond horizons and perditions, they go yonder, they do not wander. Taking care of business is a must in life. Everybody has a husband or wife. Be ye married or not or even if being single is the lot, you're worldly duties are your marriage, is this not? And if this is the desired way of being, content in this way of feeling, that is all that can be and all that should be so don't worry. But imagine if books were never written and sages were never sitting down to speak and teach the teach in. Those who feel their movement is just fine, sitting at home with libraries of books from the beginning of time, would feel bereft, and lost and bewildered, speedy steps to temple, they would be there hastily delivered. And this is why the modern sages say, these times are harder than the ancient day. Because there is so much noise and voluminous publication, posing as truth and authentic edification. And oh how lost it is, what can be said, how can it be described? Like having a billion billion when there is philosophy needed to get inside. And what you have and what you see, this is all to do and all evanescent signs that flee eventually. And when the day of foil comes where will that person go, like the track star who runs so. On that day all questions are answered, all life takes on true meaning. Until then it is only whispers, only rumors for the haggard, like a mirage in the sun, gleaming. What will come from this experience is knowing what is eminence. What do you want and you shall have it, so you have now what you have wanted in the past but take care of the habit. That quality of life that is a rut, a custom a mannerism a way of feeling learned by experience. Not by virtue or benefit of wise teaching deliverance. This is the paradox of life conditions, to be in the world and yet seek eruditions. Eruditions come when the seekers are ready, blooming like lotuses as the sun rises steady. And at night when the sun goes, where is the mind turning, where oh where it flows. Neither true fulfillment with worldly responsibilities nor truly at home with spiritual sensibilities. For there is no fruition in world or in temple. Only a dabble, never more than a fiddle. That paradox, that irony is the perennial illogicality. Of life what can be said, of the teaching what can be read? For enlightenment, the awakening of the soul in truly grand fashion. There is needed the mustering of superhuman passion. And for the seeker endowed with passion there are no further questions, only the duty to cast unremitting aspersions on ego's desires and ignorance's imaginations. And those loves, those responsibilities of life are carried on today and tonight. And these will lead to the end that loses sight. For nothing is gained, nothing is built without work aplenty. Yet all is done never to worry. Contradictions, lies, paradoxes confront the aspirant. Confusion and bewilderment make life discordant. What should I do, where shall I turn? The asking itself does indeed confirm. The compass is broken, the meter is running. And yet there are the world and home and the evanescent things, so many things coming, going once, going twice, SOLD! Who then suffers, who is struggling? Who is living, who is avoiding?

"The path of immortality is hard, and only a few find it. The rest await the Great Day when the wheels of the universe shall be stopped and the immortal sparks shall escape from the sheathes of substance. Woe unto those who wait, for they must return again, unconscious and unknowing, to the seed-ground of stars, and await a new beginning."

SMAA

END

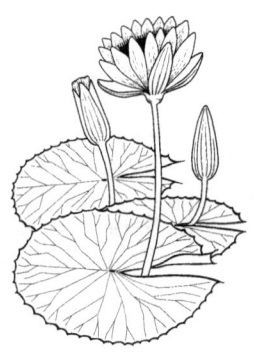

SEMA INSTITUTE

Cruzian Mystic P.O.Box 570459, Miami, Florida. 33257 (305) 378-6253, Fax. (305) 378-6253

Other Books From C M Books
P.O.Box 570459
Miami, Florida, 33257
(305) 378-6253 Fax: (305) 378-6253

This book is part of a series on the study and practice of Ancient Egyptian Yoga and Mystical Spirituality based on the writings of Dr. Muata Abhaya Ashby. They are also part of the Egyptian Yoga Course provided by the Sema Institute of Yoga. Below you will find a listing of the other books in this series. For more information send for the Egyptian Yoga Book-Audio-Video Catalog or the Egyptian Yoga Course Catalog.

Now you can study the teachings of Egyptian and Indian Yoga wisdom and Spirituality with the Egyptian Yoga Mystical Spirituality Series. The Egyptian Yoga Series takes you through the Initiation process and lead you to understand the mysteries of the soul and the Divine and to attain the highest goal of life: ENLIGHTENMENT. The *Egyptian Yoga Series*, takes you on an in depth study of Ancient Egyptian mythology and their inner mystical meaning. Each Book is prepared for the serious student of the mystical sciences and provides a study of the teachings along with exercises, assignments and projects to make the teachings understood and effective in real life. The Series is part of the Egyptian Yoga course but may be purchased even if you are not taking the course. The series is ideal for study groups.

Prices subject to change.

1. *EGYPTIAN YOGA: THE PHILOSOPHY OF ENLIGHTENMENT* An original, fully illustrated work, including hieroglyphs, detailing the meaning of the Egyptian mysteries, tantric yoga, psycho-spiritual and physical exercises. Egyptian Yoga is a guide to the practice of the highest spiritual philosophy which leads to absolute freedom from human misery and to immortality. It is well known by scholars that Egyptian philosophy is the basis of Western and Middle Eastern religious philosophies such as *Christianity, Islam, Judaism,* the *Kabala,* and Greek philosophy, but what about Indian philosophy, Yoga and Taoism? What were the original teachings? How can they be practiced today? What is the source of pain and suffering in the world and what is the solution? Discover the deepest mysteries of the mind and universe within and outside of your self. 8.5" X 11" ISBN: 1-884564-01-1 Soft $19.95

2. *EGYPTIAN YOGA: African Religion Volume 2-* Theban Theology U.S. In this long awaited sequel to *Egyptian Yoga: The Philosophy of Enlightenment* you will take a fascinating and enlightening journey back in time and discover the teachings which constituted the epitome of Ancient Egyptian spiritual wisdom. What are the disciplines which lead to the fulfillment of all desires? Delve into the three states of

consciousness (waking, dream and deep sleep) and the fourth state which transcends them all, Neberdjer, "The Absolute." These teachings of the city of Waset (Thebes) were the crowning achievement of the Sages of Ancient Egypt. They establish the standard mystical keys for understanding the profound mystical symbolism of the Triad of human consciousness. ISBN 1-884564-39-9 $23.95

3. *THE KEMETIC DIET: GUIDE TO HEALTH, DIET AND FASTING*
Health issues have always been important to human beings since the beginning of time. The earliest records of history show that the art of healing was held in high esteem since the time of Ancient Egypt. In the early 20th century, medical doctors had almost attained the status of sainthood by the promotion of the idea that they alone were "scientists" while other healing modalities and traditional healers who did not follow the "scientific method' were nothing but superstitious, ignorant charlatans who at best would take the money of their clients and at worst kill them with the unscientific "snake oils" and "irrational theories". In the late 20th century, the failure of the modern medical establishment's ability to lead the general public to good health, promoted the move by many in society towards "alternative medicine". Alternative medicine disciplines are those healing modalities which do not adhere to the philosophy of allopathic medicine. Allopathic medicine is what medical doctors practice by an large. It is the theory that disease is caused by agencies outside the body such as bacteria, viruses or physical means which affect the body. These can therefore be treated by medicines and therapies The natural healing method began in the absence of extensive technologies with the idea that all the answers for health may be found in nature or rather, the deviation from nature. Therefore, the health of the body can be restored by correcting the aberration and thereby restoring balance. This is the area that will be covered in this volume. Allopathic techniques have their place in the art of healing. However, we should not forget that the body is a grand achievement of the spirit and built into it is the capacity to maintain itself and heal itself. Ashby, Muata ISBN: 1-884564-49-6 $28.95

4. INITIATION INTO EGYPTIAN YOGA Shedy: Spiritual discipline or program, to go deeply into the mysteries, to study the mystery teachings and literature profoundly, to penetrate the mysteries. You will learn about the mysteries of initiation into the teachings and practice of Yoga and how to become an Initiate of the mystical sciences. This insightful manual is the first in a series which introduces you to the goals of daily spiritual and yoga practices: Meditation, Diet, Words of Power and the ancient wisdom teachings. 8.5" X 11" ISBN 1-884564-02-X Soft Cover $24.95 U.S.

5. *THE AFRICAN ORIGINS OF CIVILIZATION, RELIGION AND YOGA SPIRITUALITY AND ETHICS PHILOSOPHY* HARD COVER EDITION Part 1, Part 2, Part 3 in one volume 683 Pages Hard Cover First Edition Three volumes in one. Over the past several years I have been asked to put together in one volume the most important evidences showing the correlations and common teachings between Kamitan (Ancient Egyptian) culture and religion and that of India. The questions of the history of Ancient Egypt, and the latest archeological evidences

showing civilization and culture in Ancient Egypt and its spread to other countries, has intrigued many scholars as well as mystics over the years. Also, the possibility that Ancient Egyptian Priests and Priestesses migrated to Greece, India and other countries to carry on the traditions of the Ancient Egyptian Mysteries, has been speculated over the years as well. In chapter 1 of the book *Egyptian Yoga The Philosophy of Enlightenment,* 1995, I first introduced the deepest comparison between Ancient Egypt and India that had been brought forth up to that time. Now, in the year 2001 this new book, *THE AFRICAN ORIGINS OF CIVILIZATION, MYSTICAL RELIGION AND YOGA PHILOSOPHY,* more fully explores the motifs, symbols and philosophical correlations between Ancient Egyptian and Indian mysticism and clearly shows not only that Ancient Egypt and India were connected culturally but also spiritually. How does this knowledge help the spiritual aspirant? This discovery has great importance for the Yogis and mystics who follow the philosophy of Ancient Egypt and the mysticism of India. It means that India has a longer history and heritage than was previously understood. It shows that the mysteries of Ancient Egypt were essentially a yoga tradition which did not die but rather developed into the modern day systems of Yoga technology of India. It further shows that African culture developed Yoga Mysticism earlier than any other civilization in history. All of this expands our understanding of the unity of culture and the deep legacy of Yoga, which stretches into the distant past, beyond the Indus Valley civilization, the earliest known high culture in India as well as the Vedic tradition of Aryan culture. Therefore, Yoga culture and mysticism is the oldest known tradition of spiritual development and Indian mysticism is an extension of the Ancient Egyptian mysticism. By understanding the legacy which Ancient Egypt gave to India the mysticism of India is better understood and by comprehending the heritage of Indian Yoga, which is rooted in Ancient Egypt the Mysticism of Ancient Egypt is also better understood. This expanded understanding allows us to prove the underlying kinship of humanity, through the common symbols, motifs and philosophies which are not disparate and confusing teachings but in reality expressions of the same study of truth through metaphysics and mystical realization of Self. (HARD COVER) ISBN: 1-884564-50-X $45.00 U.S.   81/2" X 11"

6. *AFRICAN ORIGINS BOOK 1 PART 1* African Origins of African Civilization, Religion, Yoga Mysticism and Ethics Philosophy-Soft Cover $24.95 ISBN: 1-884564-55-0

7. *AFRICAN ORIGINS BOOK 2 PART 2* African Origins of Western Civilization, Religion and Philosophy (Soft) -Soft Cover $24.95 ISBN: 1-884564-56-9

8. *EGYPT AND INDIA AFRICAN ORIGINS OF Eastern Civilization, Religion, Yoga Mysticism and Philosophy*-Soft Cover $29.95 (Soft) ISBN: 1-884564-57-7

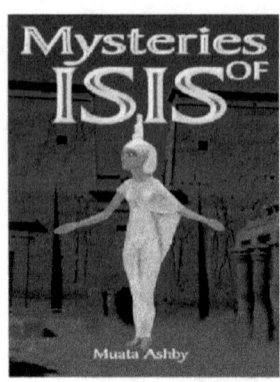

9. **THE MYSTERIES OF ISIS: The Ancient Egyptian Philosophy of Self-Realization** - There are several paths to discover the Divine and the mysteries of the higher Self. This volume details the mystery teachings of the goddess Aset (Isis) from Ancient Egypt- the path of wisdom. It includes the teachings of her temple and the disciplines that are enjoined for the initiates of the temple of Aset as they were given in ancient times. Also, this book includes the teachings of the main myths of Aset that lead a human being to spiritual enlightenment and immortality. Through the study of ancient myth and the illumination of initiatic understanding the idea of God is expanded from the mythological comprehension to the metaphysical. Then this metaphysical understanding is related to you, the student, so as to begin understanding your true divine nature. ISBN 1-884564-24-0 $22.99

10. *EGYPTIAN PROVERBS:* collection of —Ancient Egyptian Proverbs and Wisdom Teachings -How to live according to MAAT Philosophy. Beginning Meditation. All proverbs are indexed for easy searches. For the first time in one volume, ——Ancient Egyptian Proverbs, wisdom teachings and meditations, fully illustrated with hieroglyphic text and symbols. EGYPTIAN PROVERBS is a unique collection of knowledge and wisdom which you can put into practice today and transform your life. $14.95 U.S   ISBN: 1-884564-00-3

11. *GOD OF LOVE: THE PATH OF DIVINE LOVE The Process of Mystical Transformation and The Path of Divine Love*   This Volume focuses on the ancient wisdom teachings of "Neter Merri" –the Ancient Egyptian philosophy of Divine Love and how to use them in a scientific process for self-transformation. Love is one of the most powerful human emotions. It is also the source of Divine feeling that unifies God and the individual human being. When love is fragmented and diminished by egoism the Divine connection is lost. The Ancient tradition of Neter Merri leads human beings back to their Divine connection, allowing them to discover their innate glorious self that is actually Divine and immortal. This volume will detail the process of transformation from ordinary consciousness to cosmic consciousness through the integrated practice of the teachings and the path of Devotional Love toward the Divine. 5.5"x 8.5" ISBN 1-884564-11-9 $22.95

12. *INTRODUCTION TO MAAT PHILOSOPHY: Spiritual Enlightenment Through the Path of Virtue*   Known commonly as Karma in India, the teachings of MAAT contain an extensive philosophy based on ariu (deeds) and their fructification in the form of shai and renenet (fortune

and destiny, leading to Meskhenet (fate in a future birth) for living virtuously and with orderly wisdom are explained and the student is to begin practicing the precepts of Maat in daily life so as to promote the process of purification of the heart in preparation for the judgment of the soul. This judgment will be understood not as an event that will occur at the time of death but as an event that occurs continuously, at every moment in the life of the individual. The student will learn how to become allied with the forces of the Higher Self and to thereby begin cleansing the mind (heart) of impurities so as to attain a higher vision of reality. ISBN 1-884564-20-8 $22.99

13. *MEDITATION The Ancient Egyptian Path to Enlightenment*   Many people do not know about the rich history of meditation practice in Ancient Egypt. This volume outlines the theory of meditation and presents the Ancient Egyptian Hieroglyphic text which give instruction as to the nature of the mind and its three modes of expression. It also presents the texts which give instruction on the practice of meditation for spiritual Enlightenment and unity with the Divine. This volume allows the reader to begin practicing meditation by explaining, in easy to understand terms, the simplest form of meditation and working up to the most advanced form which was practiced in ancient times and which is still practiced by yogis around the world in modern times. ISBN 1-884564-27-7 $22.99

14. *THE GLORIOUS LIGHT MEDITATION* TECHNIQUE OF ANCIENT EGYPT New for the year 2000. This volume is based on the earliest known instruction in history given for the practice of formal meditation. Discovered by Dr. Muata Ashby, it is inscribed on the walls of the Tomb of Seti I in Thebes Egypt. This volume details the philosophy and practice of this unique system of meditation originated in Ancient Egypt and the earliest practice of meditation known in the world which occurred in the most advanced African Culture. ISBN: 1-884564-15-1 $16.95 (PB)

15. *THE SERPENT POWER: The Ancient Egyptian Mystical Wisdom of the Inner Life Force.* This Volume specifically deals with the latent life Force energy of the universe and in the human body, its control and sublimation. How to develop the Life Force energy of the subtle body. This Volume will introduce the esoteric wisdom of the science of how virtuous living acts in a subtle and mysterious way to cleanse the latent

psychic energy conduits and vortices of the spiritual body. ISBN 1-884564-19-4 $22.95

16.   EGYPTIAN YOGA *The Postures of The Gods and Goddesses* Discover the physical postures and exercises practiced thousands of years ago in Ancient Egypt which are today known as Yoga exercises. Discover the history of the postures and how they were transferred from Ancient Egypt in Africa to India through Buddhist Tantrism. Then practice the postures as you discover the mythic teaching that originally gave birth to the postures and was practiced by the Ancient Egyptian priests and priestesses. This work is based on the pictures and teachings from the Creation story of Ra, The Asarian Resurrection Myth and the carvings and reliefs from various Temples in Ancient Egypt 8.5" X 11" ISBN 1-884564-10-0 Soft Cover $21.95   Exercise video $20

17.   SACRED SEXUALITY: ANCIENT EGYPTIAN TANTRA YOGA: *The Art of Sex* Sublimation and Universal Consciousness This Volume will expand on the male and female principles within the human body and in the universe and further detail the sublimation of sexual energy into spiritual energy. The student will study the deities Min and Hathor, Asar and Aset, Geb and Nut and discover the mystical implications for a practical spiritual discipline. This Volume will also focus on the Tantric aspects of Ancient Egyptian and Indian mysticism, the purpose of sex and the mystical teachings of sexual sublimation which lead to self-knowledge and Enlightenment. ISBN 1-884564-03-8 $24.95

18. *AFRICAN RELIGION Volume 4: ASARIAN THEOLOGY: RESURRECTING OSIRIS* The path of Mystical Awakening and the Keys to Immortality NEW REVISED AND EXPANDED EDITION! The Ancient Sages created stories based on human and superhuman beings whose struggles, aspirations, needs and desires ultimately lead them to discover their true Self. The myth of Aset, Asar and Heru is no exception in this area. While there is no one source where the entire story may be found, pieces of it are inscribed in various ancient Temples walls, tombs, steles and papyri. For the first time available, the complete myth of Asar, Aset and Heru has been compiled from original Ancient Egyptian, Greek and Coptic Texts. This epic myth has been richly illustrated with reliefs from the Temple of Heru at Edfu, the Temple of Aset at Philae, the Temple of Asar at Abydos, the Temple of Hathor at Denderah and various papyri, inscriptions and reliefs. Discover the myth which inspired the teachings of the *Shetaut Neter* (Egyptian Mystery System - Egyptian Yoga) and the Egyptian Book of Coming Forth By Day. Also, discover the three levels of Ancient Egyptian Religion, how to understand the mysteries of the Duat or Astral World and how to discover the abode of the Supreme in the Amenta, *The Other World* The ancient religion of Asar, Aset and Heru, if properly understood, contains all of the elements necessary to lead the sincere aspirant to attain immortality through inner self-discovery. This volume presents the entire myth and explores the main mystical themes and rituals associated with the myth for understating human existence, creation and the way to achieve spiritual emancipation - *Resurrection.* The Asarian myth is so powerful that it influenced and is still having an effect on the major world religions. Discover the origins and mystical meaning of the Christian Trinity, the Eucharist ritual and the ancient origin of the birthday of Jesus Christ. Soft Cover ISBN: 1-884564-27-5 $24.95

19. ***THE EGYPTIAN BOOK OF THE DEAD MYSTICISM OF THE PERT EM HERU*** " I Know myself, I know myself, I am One With God!– From the Pert Em Heru "The Ru Pert em Heru" or "Ancient Egyptian Book of The Dead," or "Book of Coming Forth By Day" as it is more popularly known, has fascinated the world since the successful translation of Ancient Egyptian hieroglyphic scripture over 150 years ago. The astonishing writings in it reveal that the Ancient Egyptians believed in life after death and in an ultimate destiny to discover the Divine. The elegance and aesthetic beauty of the hieroglyphic text itself has inspired many see it as an art form in and of itself. But is there more to it than that? Did the Ancient Egyptian wisdom contain more than just aphorisms and hopes of eternal life beyond death? In this volume Dr. Muata Ashby, the author of over 25 books on Ancient Egyptian Yoga Philosophy has produced a new translation of the original texts which uncovers a mystical teaching underlying the sayings and rituals instituted by the Ancient Egyptian Sages and Saints. "Once the philosophy of Ancient Egypt is understood as a mystical tradition instead of as a religion or primitive mythology, it reveals its secrets which if practiced today will lead anyone to discover the glory of spiritual self-discovery. The Pert em Heru is in every way comparable to the Indian Upanishads or the Tibetan Book of the Dead." $28.95   ISBN# 1-884564-28-3 Size: 8½" X 11

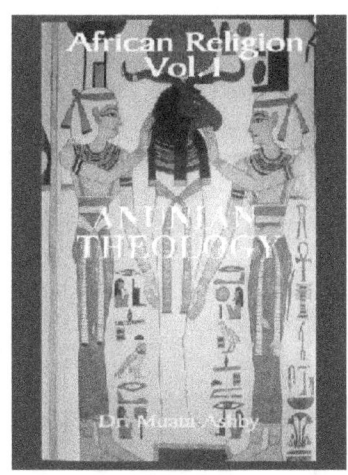

20. *African Religion VOL. 1- ANUNIAN THEOLOGY THE MYSTERIES OF RA* The Philosophy of Anu and The Mystical Teachings of The Ancient Egyptian Creation Myth Discover the mystical teachings contained in the Creation Myth and the gods and goddesses who brought creation and human beings into existence. The Creation myth of Anu is the source of Anunian Theology but also of the other main theological systems of Ancient Egypt that also influenced other world religions including Christianity, Hinduism and Buddhism. The Creation Myth holds the key to understanding the universe and for attaining spiritual Enlightenment. ISBN: 1-884564-38-0 $19.95

21. *African Religion VOL 3: Memphite Theology: MYSTERIES OF MIND* Mystical Psychology & Mental Health for Enlightenment and Immortality based on the Ancient Egyptian Philosophy of Menefer - Mysticism of Ptah, Egyptian Physics and Yoga Metaphysics and the Hidden properties of Matter.   This volume uncovers the mystical psychology of the Ancient Egyptian wisdom teachings centering on the philosophy of the Ancient Egyptian city of Menefer (Memphite

Theology). How to understand the mind and how to control the senses and lead the mind to health, clarity and mystical self-discovery. This Volume will also go deeper into the philosophy of God as creation and will explore the concepts of modern science and how they correlate with ancient teachings. This Volume will lay the ground work for the understanding of the philosophy of universal consciousness and the initiatic/yogic insight into who or what is God? ISBN 1-884564-07-0 $22.95

22. *AFRICAN RELIGION VOLUME 5: THE GODDESS AND THE EGYPTIAN MYSTERIESTHE PATH OF THE GODDESS THE GODDESS PATH* The Secret Forms of the Goddess and the Rituals of Resurrection The Supreme Being may be worshipped as father or as mother. *Ushet Rekhat* or *Mother Worship*, is the spiritual process of worshipping the Divine in the form of the Divine Goddess. It celebrates the most important forms of the Goddess including *Nathor, Maat, Aset, Arat, Amentet and Hathor* and explores their mystical meaning as well as the rising of *Sirius,* the star of Aset (Aset) and the new birth of Hor (Heru). The end of the year is a time of reckoning, reflection and engendering a new or renewed positive movement toward attaining spiritual Enlightenment. The Mother Worship devotional meditation ritual, performed on five days during the month of December and on New Year's Eve, is based on the Ushet Rekhit. During the ceremony, the cosmic forces, symbolized by Sirius - and the constellation of Orion ---, are harnessed through the understanding and devotional attitude of the participant. This propitiation draws the light of wisdom and health to all those who share in the ritual, leading to prosperity and wisdom. $14.95 ISBN 1-884564-18-6

23. **THE MYSTICAL JOURNEY FROM JESUS TO CHRIST** Discover the ancient Egyptian origins of Christianity before the Catholic Church and learn the mystical teachings given by Jesus to assist all humanity in becoming Christlike. Discover the secret meaning of the Gospels that were discovered in Egypt. Also discover how and why so many Christian churches came into being. Discover that the Bible still holds the keys to mystical realization even though its original writings were changed by the church. Discover how to practice the original teachings of Christianity which leads to the Kingdom of Heaven. $24.95 ISBN# 1-884564-05-4 size: 8½" X 11"

24. **THE STORY OF ASAR, ASET AND HERU:** An Ancient Egyptian Legend (For Children)   Now for the first time, the most ancient myth of Ancient Egypt comes alive for children. Inspired by the books *The Asarian Resurrection: The Ancient Egyptian Bible* and *The Mystical Teachings of The Asarian Resurrection, The Story of Asar, Aset and Heru* is an easy to understand and thrilling tale which inspired the children of Ancient Egypt to aspire to greatness and righteousness. If you and your child have enjoyed stories like *The Lion King* and *Star Wars you will love The Story of Asar, Aset and Heru.* Also, if you know

the story of Jesus and Krishna you will discover than Ancient Egypt had a similar myth and that this myth carries important spiritual teachings for living a fruitful and fulfilling life. This book may be used along with *The Parents Guide To The Asarian Resurrection Myth: How to Teach Yourself and Your Child the Principles of Universal Mystical Religion.* The guide provides some background to the Asarian Resurrection myth and it also gives insight into the mystical teachings contained in it which you may introduce to your child. It is designed for parents who wish to grow spiritually with their children and it serves as an introduction for those who would like to study the Asarian Resurrection Myth in depth and to practice its teachings. 8.5" X 11" ISBN: 1-884564-31-3 $12.95

25.   *THE PARENTS GUIDE TO THE AUSARIAN RESURRECTION MYTH:* How to Teach Yourself and Your Child the Principles of Universal Mystical Religion.   This insightful manual brings for the timeless wisdom of the ancient through the Ancient Egyptian myth of Asar, Aset and Heru and the mystical teachings contained in it for parents who want to guide their children to understand and practice the teachings of mystical spirituality. This manual may be used with the children's storybook *The Story of Asar, Aset and Heru* by Dr. Muata Abhaya Ashby.   ISBN: 1-884564-30-5 $16.95

26. *HEALING THE CRIMINAL HEART.* Introduction to Maat Philosophy, Yoga and Spiritual Redemption Through the Path of Virtue Who is a criminal? Is there such a thing as a criminal heart? What is the source of evil and sinfulness and is there any way to rise above it? Is there redemption for those who have committed sins, even the worst crimes? Ancient Egyptian mystical psychology holds important answers to these questions. Over ten thousand years ago mystical psychologists, the Sages of Ancient Egypt, studied and charted the human mind and spirit and laid out a path which will lead to spiritual redemption, prosperity and Enlightenment.   This introductory volume brings forth the teachings of the Asarian Resurrection, the most important myth of Ancient Egypt, with relation to the faults of human existence: anger, hatred, greed, lust, animosity, discontent, ignorance, egoism jealousy, bitterness, and a myriad of psycho-spiritual ailments which keep a human being in a state of negativity and adversity   ISBN: 1-884564-17-8 $15.95

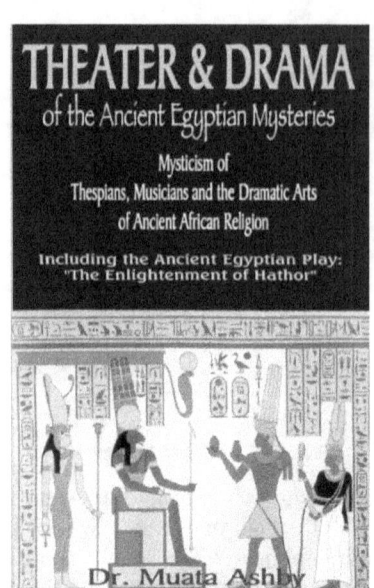

27. **TEMPLE RITUAL OF THE ANCIENT EGYPTIAN MYSTERIES-- THEATER & DRAMA OF THE ANCIENT EGYPTIAN MYSTERIES**: Details the practice of the mysteries and ritual program of the temple and the philosophy an practice of the ritual of the mysteries, its purpose and execution. Featuring the Ancient Egyptian stage play-"The Enlightenment of Hathor' Based on an Ancient Egyptian Drama, The original Theater -Mysticism of the Temple of Hetheru 1-884564-14-3 $19.95 By Dr. Muata Ashby

28. *GUIDE TO PRINT ON DEMAND: SELF-PUBLISH FOR PROFIT,* SPIRITUAL FULFILLMENT AND SERVICE TO HUMANITY Everyone asks us how we produced so many books in such a short time. Here are the secrets to writing and producing books that uplift humanity and how to get them printed for a fraction of the regular cost. Anyone can become an author even if they have limited funds. All that is necessary is the willingness to learn how the printing and book business work and the desire to follow the special instructions given here for preparing your manuscript format. Then you take your work directly to the non-traditional companies who can produce your books for less than the traditional book printer can. ISBN: 1-884564-40-2 $16.95 U. S.

29. *Egyptian Mysteries: Vol. 1,* Shetaut Neter What are the Mysteries? For thousands of years the spiritual tradition of Ancient Egypt, S*hetaut Neter,* "The Egyptian Mysteries," "The Secret Teachings," have fascinated, tantalized and amazed the world. At one time exalted and recognized as the highest culture of the world, by Africans, Europeans, Asiatics, Hindus, Buddhists and other cultures of the ancient world, in time it was shunned by the emerging orthodox world religions. Its temples desecrated, its philosophy maligned, its tradition spurned, its philosophy dormant in the mystical *Medu Neter,* the mysterious hieroglyphic texts which hold the secret symbolic meaning that has scarcely been discerned up to now. What are the secrets of *Nehast* {spiritual awakening and emancipation, resurrection}. More than just a literal translation, this volume is for awakening to the secret code *Shetitu* of the teaching which was not deciphered by Egyptologists, nor could be understood by ordinary spiritualists. This book is a reinstatement of the original science made available for our times, to the reincarnated followers of Ancient Egyptian culture and the prospect of spiritual freedom to break the bonds of *Khemn,* "ignorance," and slavery to evil forces: *Såaa* . ISBN: 1-884564-41-0 $19.99

30. *EGYPTIAN MYSTERIES VOL 2:* Dictionary of Gods and Goddesses This book is about the mystery of neteru, the gods and goddesses of Ancient Egypt (Kamit, Kemet). Neteru means "Gods and Goddesses." But the Neterian teaching of Neteru represents more than the usual limited modern day concept of "divinities" or "spirits." The Neteru of Kamit are also metaphors, cosmic principles and vehicles for the enlightening teachings of Shetaut Neter (Ancient Egyptian-African Religion). Actually they are the elements for one of the most advanced systems of spirituality ever conceived in human history. Understanding the concept of neteru provides a firm basis for spiritual evolution and the pathway for viable culture, peace on earth and a healthy human society.   Why is it important to have gods and goddesses in our lives? In order for spiritual evolution to be possible, once a human being has accepted that there is existence after death and there is a transcendental being who exists beyond time and space knowledge, human beings

need a connection to that which transcends the ordinary experience of human life in time and space and a means to understand the transcendental reality beyond the mundane reality. ISBN: 1-884564-23-2 $21.95

31. *EGYPTIAN MYSTERIES VOL. 3* The Priests and Priestesses of Ancient Egypt This volume details the path of Neterian priesthood, the joys, challenges and rewards of advanced Neterian life, the teachings that allowed the priests and priestesses to manage the most long lived civilization in human history and how that path can be adopted today; for those who want to tread the path of the Clergy of Shetaut Neter. ISBN: 1-884564-53-4 $24.95

32. *The War of Heru and Set:* The Struggle of Good and Evil for Control of the World and The Human Soul This volume contains a novelized version of the Asarian Resurrection myth that is based on the actual scriptures presented in the Book Asarian Religion (old name – Resurrecting Osiris). This volume is prepared in the form of a screenplay and can be easily adapted to be used as a stage play. Spiritual seeking is a mythic journey that has many emotional highs and lows, ecstasies and depressions, victories and frustrations. This is the War of Life that is played out in the myth as the struggle of Heru and Set and those are mythic characters that represent the human

Higher and Lower self. How to understand the war and emerge victorious in the journey o life? The ultimate victory and fulfillment can be experienced, which is not changeable or lost in time. The purpose of myth is to convey the wisdom of life through the story of divinities who show the way to overcome the challenges and foibles of life. In this volume the feelings and emotions of the characters of the myth have been highlighted to show the deeply rich texture of the Ancient Egyptian myth. This myth contains deep spiritual teachings and insights into the nature of self, of God and the mysteries of life and the means to discover the true meaning of life and thereby achieve the true purpose of life. To become victorious in the battle of life means to become the King (or Queen) of Egypt.Have you seen movies like The Lion King, Hamlet, The Odyssey, or The Little Buddha? These have been some of the most popular movies in modern times. The Sema Institute of Yoga is dedicated to researching and presenting the wisdom and culture of ancient Africa. The Script is designed to be produced as a motion picture but may be addapted for the theater as well. $21.95 copyright 1998 By Dr. Muata Ashby ISBN 1-8840564-44-5

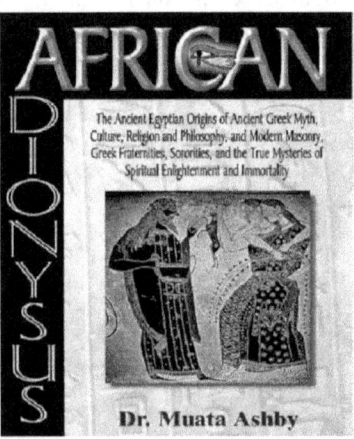

33. *AFRICAN DIONYSUS: FROM EGYPT TO GREECE:* The Kamitan Origins of Greek Culture and Religion ISBN: 1-884564-47-X FROM EGYPT TO GREECE This insightful manual is a reference to Ancient Egyptian mythology and philosophy and its correlation to what later became known as Greek and Rome mythology and philosophy. It outlines the basic tenets of the mythologies and shoes the ancient origins of Greek culture in Ancient Egypt. This volume also documents the origins of the Greek alphabet in Egypt as well as Greek religion, myth and philosophy of the gods and goddesses from Egypt from the myth of Atlantis and archaic period with the Minoans to the Classical period. This volume also acts as a resource for Colleges students who would like to set up fraternities and sororities based on the original

Ancient Egyptian principles of Sheti and Maat philosophy. ISBN: 1-884564-47-X $22.95 U.S.

34. *THE FORTY TWO PRECEPTS OF MAAT, THE PHILOSOPHY OF RIGHTEOUS ACTION AND THE ANCIENT EGYPTIAN WISDOM TEXTS* <u>ADVANCED STUDIES</u> This manual is designed for use with the 1998 Maat Philosophy Class conducted by Dr. Muata Ashby. This is a detailed study of Maat Philosophy. It contains a compilation of the 42 laws or precepts of Maat and the corresponding principles which they represent along with the teachings of the ancient Egyptian Sages relating to each. Maat philosophy was the basis of Ancient Egyptian society and government as well as the heart of Ancient Egyptian myth and spirituality. Maat is at once a goddess, a cosmic force and a living social doctrine, which promotes social harmony and thereby paves the way for spiritual evolution in all levels of society. ISBN: 1-884564-48-8 $16.95 U.S.

35. THE SECRET LOTUS: *Poetry of Enlightenment*
Discover the mystical sentiment of the Kemetic teaching as expressed through the poetry of Sebai Muata Ashby. The teaching of spiritual awakening is uniquely experienced when the poetic sensibility is present. This first volume contains the poems written between 1996 and 2003. **1-884564--16 -X $16.99**

36. The Ancient Egyptian Buddha: The Ancient Egyptian Origins of Buddhism

This book is a compilation of several sections of a larger work, a book by the name of African Origins of Civilization, Religion, Yoga Mysticism and Ethics Philosophy. It also contains some additional evidences not contained in the larger work that demonstrate the correlation between Ancient Egyptian Religion and Buddhism. This book is one of several compiled short volumes that has been compiled so as to facilitate access to specific subjects contained in the larger work which is over 680 pages long. These short and small volumes have been specifically designed to cover one subject in a brief and low cost format. This present volume, The Ancient Egyptian Buddha: The Ancient Egyptian Origins of Buddhism, formed one subject in the larger work; actually it was one chapter of the larger work. However, this volume has some new additional evidences and comparisons of Buddhist and Neterian (Ancient Egyptian) philosophies not previously discussed. It was felt that this subject needed to be discussed because even in the early 21st century, the idea persists that Buddhism originated only in India independently. Yet there is ample evidence from ancient writings and perhaps more importantly, iconographical evidences from the Ancient Egyptians and early Buddhists themselves that prove otherwise. This handy volume has been designed to be accessible to young adults and all others who would like to have an easy reference with documentation on this important subject. This is an important subject because the frame of reference with which we look at a culture depends strongly on our conceptions about its origins. in this case, if we look at the Buddhism as an Asiatic religion we would treat it and it's culture in one way. If we id as African [Ancient Egyptian] we not only would see it in a different light but we also must ascribe Africa with a glorious legacy that matches any other culture in human history and gave rise to one of the present day most important religious philosophies. We would also look at the culture and philosophies of the Ancient Egyptians as having African insights that offer us greater depth into the Buddhist philosophies. Those insights inform our knowledge about other African traditions and we can also begin to understand in a deeper way the effect of Ancient Egyptian culture on African culture and also on the Asiatic as well. We would also be able to discover the glorious and wondrous teaching of mystical philosophy that Ancient Egyptian Shetaut Neter religion offers, that is as powerful as any other mystic system of spiritual philosophy in the world today. ISBN: 1-884564-61-5 $28.95

37. The Death of American Empire: Neo-conservatism, Theocracy, Economic Imperialism, Environmental Disaster and the Collapse of Civilization

This work is a collection of essays relating to social and economic, leadership, and ethics, ecological and religious issues that are facing the world today in order to understand the course of history that has led humanity to its present condition and then arrive at positive solutions that will lead to better outcomes for all humanity. It surveys the development and decline of major empires throughout history and focuses on the creation of American Empire along with the social, political and economic policies that led to the prominence of the United States of America as a Superpower including the rise of the political control of the neo-con political philosophy including militarism and the military industrial complex in American politics and the rise of the religious right into and American Theocracy movement. This volume details, through historical and current events, the psychology behind the dominance of western culture in world politics through the "Superpower Syndrome Mandatory Conflict Complex" that drives the Superpower culture to establish itself above all others and then act hubristically to dominate world culture through legitimate influences as well as coercion, media censorship and misinformation leading to international hegemony and world conflict. This volume also details the financial policies that gave rise to American prominence in the global economy, especially after World War II, and promoted American preeminence over the world economy through Globalization as well as the environmental policies, including the oil economy, that are promoting degradation of the world ecology and contribute to the decline of America as an Empire culture. This volume finally explores the factors pointing to the decline of the American Empire economy and imperial power and what to expect in the aftermath of American prominence and how to survive the decline while at the same time promoting policies and social-economic-religious-political changes that are needed in order to promote the emergence of a beneficial and sustainable culture. **$25.95soft** 1-884564-25-9, Hard Cover **$29.95soft** 1-884564-45-3

38. The African Origins of Hatha Yoga: And its Ancient Mystical Teaching

The subject of this present volume, The Ancient Egyptian Origins of Yoga Postures, formed one subject in the larger works, African Origins of Civilization Religion, Yoga Mysticism and Ethics Philosophy and the Book Egypt and India is the section of the book African Origins of Civilization. Those works contain the collection of all correlations between Ancient Egypt and India. This volume also contains some additional information not contained in the previous work. It was felt that this subject needed to be discussed more directly, being treated in one volume, as opposed to being contained in the larger work along with other subjects, because even in the early 21st century, the idea persists that the Yoga and specifically, Yoga Postures, were invented and developed only in India. The Ancient Egyptians were peoples originally from Africa who were, in ancient times, colonists in India. Therefore it is no surprise that many Indian traditions including religious and Yogic, would be found earlier in Ancient Egypt. Yet there is ample evidence from ancient writings and perhaps more importantly, iconographical evidences from the Ancient Egyptians themselves and the Indians themselves that prove the connection between Ancient Egypt and India as well as the existence of a discipline of Yoga Postures in Ancient Egypt long before its practice in India. This handy volume has been designed to be accessible to young adults and all others who would like to have an easy reference with documentation on this important subject. This is an important subject because the frame of reference with which we look at a culture depends strongly on our conceptions about its origins. In this case, if we look at the Ancient Egyptians as Asiatic peoples we would treat them and their culture in one way. If we see them as Africans we not only see them in a different light but we also must ascribe Africa with a glorious legacy that matches any other culture in human history. We would also look at the culture and philosophies of the Ancient Egyptians as having African insights instead of Asiatic ones. Those insights inform our knowledge bout other African traditions and we can also begin to understand in a deeper way the effect of Ancient Egyptian culture on African culture and also on the Asiatic as well. When we discover the deeper and more ancient practice of the postures system in Ancient Egypt that was called "Hatha Yoga" in India, we are able to find a new and expanded understanding of the practice that constitutes a discipline of spiritual practice that informs and revitalizes the Indian practices as well as all spiritual disciplines. $19.99 ISBN 1-884564-60-7

39. The Black Ancient Egyptians

This present volume, The Black Ancient Egyptians: The Black African Ancestry of the Ancient Egyptians, formed one subject in the larger work: The African Origins of Civilization, Religion, Yoga Mysticism and Ethics Philosophy. It was felt that this subject needed to be discussed because even in the early 21st century, the idea persists that the Ancient Egyptians were peoples originally from Asia Minor who came into North-East Africa. Yet there is ample evidence from ancient writings and perhaps more importantly, iconographical evidences from the Ancient Egyptians themselves that proves otherwise. This handy volume has been designed to be accessible to young adults and all others who would like to have an easy reference with documentation on this important subject. This is an important subject because the frame of reference with which we look at a culture depends strongly on our conceptions about its origins. in this case, if we look at the Ancient Egyptians as Asiatic peoples we would treat them and their culture in one way. If we see them as Africans we not only see them in a different light but we also must ascribe Africa with a glorious legacy that matches any other culture in human history. We would also look at the culture and philosophies of the Ancient Egyptians as having African insights instead of Asiatic ones. Those insights inform our knowledge bout other African traditions and we can also begin to understand in a deeper way the effect of Ancient Egyptian culture on African culture and also on the Asiatic as well. ISBN 1-884564-21-6 $19.99

40. The Limits of Faith: The Failure of Faith-based Religions and the Solution to the Meaning of Life

Is faith belief in something without proof? And if so is there never to be any proof or discovery? If so what is the need of intellect? If faith is trust in something that is real is that reality historical, literal or metaphorical or philosophical? If knowledge is an essential element in faith why should there by so much emphasis on believing and not on understanding in the modern practice of religion? This volume is a compilation of essays related to the nature of religious faith in the context of its inception in human history as well as its meaning for religious practice and relations between religions in modern times.

Faith has come to be regarded as a virtuous goal in life. However, many people have asked how can it be that an endeavor that is supposed to be dedicated to spiritual upliftment has led to more conflict in human history than any other social factor? ISBN 1884564631 SOFT COVER - $19.99, ISBN 1884564623 HARD COVER -$28.95

41. **Redemption of The Criminal Heart Through Kemetic Spirituality and Maat Philosophy**
Special book dedicated to inmates, their families and members of the Law Enforcement community. ISBN: 1-884564-70-4
$5.00

42. COMPARATIVE MYTHOLOGY
What are Myth and Culture and what is their importance for understanding the

development of societies, human evolution and the search for meaning? What is the purpose of culture and how do cultures evolve? What are the elements of a culture and how can those elements be broken down and the constituent parts of a culture understood and compared? How do cultures interact? How does enculturation occur and how do people interact with other cultures? How do the processes of acculturation and cooptation occur and what does this mean for the development of a society? How can the study of myths and the elements of culture help in understanding the meaning of life and the means to promote understanding and peace in the world of human activity? This volume is the exposition of a method for studying and comparing cultures, myths and other social aspects of a society. It is an expansion on the Cultural Category Factor Correlation method for studying and comparing myths, cultures, religions and other aspects of human culture. It was originally introduced in the year 2002. This volume contains an expanded treatment as well as several refinements along with examples of the application of the method. the apparent. I hope you enjoy these art renditions as serene reflections of the mysteries of life. ISBN: 1-884564-72-0
Book price $21.95

43. CONVERSATION WITH GOD: Revelations of the Important Questions of Life
$24.99 U.S.

This volume contains a grouping of some of the questions that have been submitted to Sebai Dr. Muata Ashby. They are efforts by many aspirants to better understand and practice the teachings of mystical spirituality. It is said that when sages are asked spiritual questions they are relaying the wisdom of God, the Goddess, the Higher Self, etc. There is a very special quality about the Q & A process that does not occur during a regular lecture session. Certain points come out that would not come out otherwise due to the nature of the process which ideally occurs after a lecture. Having been to a certain degree enlightened by a lecture certain new questions arise and the answers to these have the effect of elevating the teaching of the lecture to even higher levels. Therefore, enjoy these exchanges and may they lead you to enlightenment, peace and prosperity. Available Late Summer 2007 ISBN: 1-884564-68-2

44. **MYSTIC ART PAINTINGS**
(with Full Color images) This book contains a collection of the small number of paintings that I have created over the years. Some were used as early book covers and others were done simply to express certain spiritual feelings; some were created for no purpose except to express the joy of color and the feeling of relaxed freedom. All are to elicit mystical awakening in the viewer. Writing a book on philosophy is like sculpture, the more the work is rewritten the reflections and ideas become honed and take form and become clearer and imbued with intellectual beauty. Mystic music is like meditation, a world of its own that exists about 1 inch above ground wherein the musician does not touch the ground. Mystic Graphic Art is meditation in form, color, image and reflected image which opens the door to the reality behind the apparent. I hope you enjoy these art renditions and my reflections on them as serene reflections of the mysteries of life, as visual renditions of the philosophy I have written about over the years. ISBN 1-884564-69-0 $19.95

45. ANCIENT EGYPTIAN HIEROGLYPHS FOR BEGINNERS
This brief guide was prepared for those inquiring about how to enter into Hieroglyphic studies on their own at home or in study groups. First of all you should know that there are a few institutions around the world which teach how to read the Hieroglyphic text but due to the nature of the study there are perhaps only a handful of people who can read fluently. It is possible for anyone with average intelligence to achieve a high level of proficiency in reading inscriptions on temples and artifacts; however, reading extensive texts is another issue entirely. However, this introduction will give you entry into those texts if assisted by dictionaries and other aids. Most Egyptologists have a basic knowledge and keep dictionaries and notes handy when it comes to dealing with more difficult texts. Medtu Neter or the Ancient Egyptian hieroglyphic language has been considered as a "Dead Language." However, dead languages have always been studied by individuals who for the most part have taught themselves through various means. This book will discuss those means and how to use them most efficiently. ISBN 1884564429 **$28.95**

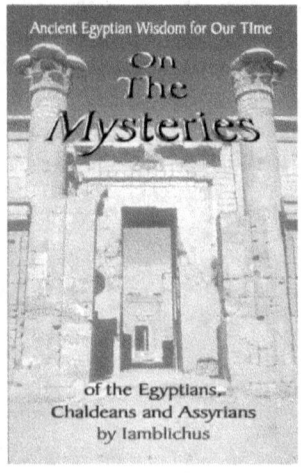

46. ON THE MYSTERIES: Wisdom of An Ancient Egyptian Sage -with Foreword by Muata Ashby

This volume, On the Mysteries, by Iamblichus (Abamun) is a unique form or scripture out of the Ancient Egyptian religious tradition. It is written in a form that is not usual or which is not usually found in the remnants of Ancient Egyptian scriptures. It is in the form of teacher and disciple, much like the Eastern scriptures such as Bhagavad Gita or the Upanishads. This form of writing may not have been necessary in Ancient times, because the format of teaching in Egypt was different prior to the conquest period by the Persians, Assyrians, Greeks and later the Romans. The question and answer format can be found but such extensive discourses and corrections of misunderstandings within the context of a teacher - disciple relationship is not usual. It therefore provides extensive insights into the times when it was written and the state of practice of Ancient Egyptian and other mystery religions. This has important implications for our times because we are today, as in the Greco-Roman period, also besieged with varied religions and new age philosophies as well as social strife and war. How can we understand our times and also make sense of the forest of spiritual traditions? How can we cut through the cacophony of religious fanaticism, and ignorance as well as misconceptions about the mysteries on the other in order to discover the true purpose of religion and the secret teachings that open up the mysteries of life and the way to enlightenment and immortality? This book, which comes to us from so long ago, offers us transcendental wisdom that applied to the world two thousand years ago as well as our world today. ISBN 1-884564-64-X $25.95

47. The Ancient Egyptian Wisdom Texts -Compiled by Muata Ashby

The Ancient Egyptian Wisdom Texts are a genre of writings from the ancient culture that have survived to the present and provide a vibrant record of the practice of spiritual evolution otherwise known as religion or yoga philosophy in Ancient Egypt. The principle focus of the Wisdom Texts is the cultivation of understanding, peace, harmony, selfless service, self-control, Inner fulfillment and spiritual realization. When these factors are cultivated in human life, the virtuous qualities in a human being begin to manifest and sinfulness, ignorance and negativity diminish until a person is able to enter into higher consciousness, the coveted goal of all civilizations. It is this virtuous mode of life which opens the door to self-discovery and spiritual enlightenment. Therefore, the Wisdom Texts are important scriptures on the subject of human nature, spiritual psychology and mystical philosophy. The teachings presented in the Wisdom Texts form the foundation of religion as well as the guidelines for conducting the affairs of every area of social interaction including commerce, education, the army, marriage, and especially the legal system. These texts were sources for the famous 42 Precepts of Maat of the Pert M Heru (Book of the Dead), essential regulations of good conduct to develop virtue and purity in order to attain higher consciousness and immortality after death. ISBN1-884564-65-8 $18.95

48. THE KEMETIC TREE OF LIFE
THE KEMETIC TREE OF LIFE: Newly Revealed Ancient Egyptian Cosmology and Metaphysics for Higher Consciousness The Tree of Life is a roadmap of a journey which explains how Creation came into being and how it will end. It also explains what Creation is composed of and also what human beings are and what they are composed of. It also explains the process of Creation, how Creation develops, as well as who created Creation and where that entity may be found. It also explains how a human being may discover that entity and in so doing also discover the secrets of Creation, the meaning of life and the means to break free from the pathetic condition of human limitation and mortality in order to discover the higher realms of being by discovering the principles, the levels of existence that are beyond the simple physical and material aspects of life. This book contains color plates   **ISBN: 1-884564-74-7 $27.95 U.S.**

49-MATRIX OF AFRICAN PROVERBS: The Ethical and Spiritual Blueprint
This volume sets forth the fundamental principles of African ethics and their practical applications for use by individuals and organizations seeking to model their ethical policies using the Traditional African values and concepts of ethical human behavior for the proper sustenance and management of society. Furthermore, this book will provide guidance as to how the Traditional African Ethics may be viewed and applied, taking into consideration the technological and social advancements in the present. This volume also presents the principles of ethical culture, and references for each to specific injunctions from Traditional African Proverbial Wisdom Teachings. These teachings are compiled from varied Pre-colonial African societies including Yoruba, Ashanti, Kemet, Malawi, Nigeria, Ethiopia, Galla, Ghana and many more. ISBN 1-884564-77-1

50- **Growing Beyond Hate: Keys to Freedom from Discord, Racism, Sexism, Political Conflict, Class Warfare, Violence, and How to Achieve Peace and Enlightenment**---INTRODUCTION: WHY DO WE HATE? Hatred is one of the fundamental motivating aspects of human life; the other is desire. Desire can be of a worldly nature or of a spiritual, elevating nature. Worldly desire and hatred are like two sides of the same coin in that human life is usually swaying from one to the other; but the question is why? And is there a way to satisfy the desiring or hating mind in such a way as to find peace in life? Why do human beings go to war? Why do human beings perpetrate violence against one another? And is there a way not just to understand the phenomena but to resolve the issues that plague humanity and could lead to a more harmonious society? Hatred is perhaps the greatest scourge of humanity in that it leads to misunderstanding, conflict and untold miseries of life and clashes between individuals, societies and nations. Therefore, the riddle of Hatred, that is, understanding the sources of it and how to confront, reduce and even eradicate it so as to bring forth the fulfillment in life and peace for society, should be a top priority for social scientists, spiritualists and philosophers. This book is written from the perspective of spiritual philosophy based on the mystical wisdom and sema or yoga philosophy of the Ancient Egyptians. This philosophy, originated and based in the wisdom of Shetaut Neter, the Egyptian Mysteries, and Maat, ethical way of life in society and in spirit, contains Sema-Yogic wisdom and understanding of life's predicaments that can allow a human being of any ethnic group to understand and overcome the causes of hatred, racism, sexism, violence and disharmony in life, that plague human society. ISBN: 1-884564-81-X

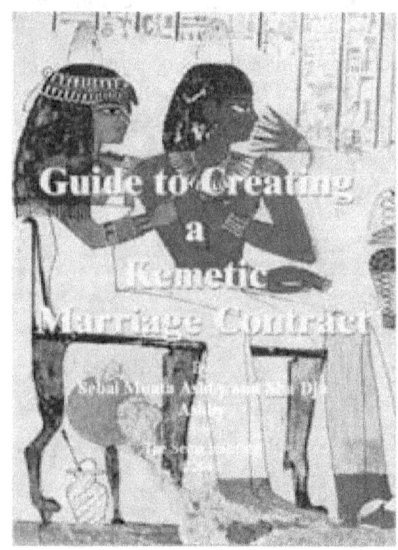

52. Guide to Creating a Kemetic Marriage Contract

This marital contract guide reflects actual Ancient Egyptian Principles for Kemetic Marriage as they are to be applied for our times. The marital contract allows people to have a framework with which to face the challenges of marital relations instead of relying on hopes or romantic dreams that everything will workout somehow; in other words, love is not all you need. The latter is not an evolved, mature way of handling one of the most important aspects of human life. Therefore, it behooves anyone who wishes to enter into a marriage to explore the issues, express their needs and seek to avoid costly mistakes, and resolve conflicts in the normal course of life or make sure that their rights and dignity will be protected if any eventuality should occur. Marital relations in Ancient Egypt were not like those in other countries of the time and not like those of present day countries. The extreme longevity of Ancient Egyptian society, founded in Maat philosophy, allowed the social development of marriage to evolve and progress to a high level of order and balance. Maat represents truth, righteous, justice and harmony in life. This meant that the marital partner's rights were to be protected with equal standing before the law. So there was no disparity between rights of men or rights of women. Therefore, anyone who wants to enter into a marriage based on Kemetic principles must first and foremost adhere to this standard…equality in the rights of men and women. This guide demonstrates procedures for following the Ancient Egyptian practice of formalizing marriage with a contract that spells out the important concerns of each partner in the marital relationship, based on Maatian principles [of righteous, truth, harmony and justice] so that the rights and needs of each partner may be protected within the marriage. It also allows the partners to think about issues that arise out of the marital relations so that they may have a foundation to fall back on in the event that those or other unforeseen issues arise and cause conflict in the relationship. By having a document of expressed concerns, needs and steps to be taken to address them, it is less likely that issues which affect the

relationship in a negative way will arise, and when they do, they will be better handled, in a more balanced, just and amicable way.
EBOOK ISBN 978-1-937016-59-3, HARDCOPY BOOK ISBN: 1-884564-82-8

53. Guide for Aspirants Seeking Asaru Initiation

This is a primer on initiatic science. Explains the journey of initiation and the levels of initiation, the reason for the need of having a preceptor and the qualities an aspirant needs to display in order to be qualified for Asaru initiation. What specific disciplines are to be practiced The Asaru initiation or Temple initiation is the level of initiation where an aspirant is given certain secret knowledge for activating the subtle body in order to discover higher planes of being and higher essence of Self. ANSWERS

THE QUESTIONS: 1. Why Are there Three Main Levels of Initiation? And How do they relate to the levels of initiation and the levels of initiatic teachings that are imparted? 2. HOW TO UNDERSTAND THE RELATION BETWEEN THE LEVELS OF INITIATION, THE ROLE OF THE TEACHER DISCIPLE RELATIONSHIP AND THE GOAL OF INITIATION 3. WHAT IS THE RELATIVE VALUE OF THE SHEMS LEVEL OF INITIATION IN REFERENCE TO THE ASAR LEVEL AND WHY DOES THE TEMPLE USE A HIERARCHICAL STRUCTURE FOR DELIVERING THE TEACHINGS? 4. WHY IS THE DEMARCATION MADE BETWEEN THE SHEMS LEVEL AND ASARU LEVEL OF ASPIRANTS? 5. WHAT IS COMPASSION IN THE INITIATIC SCIENCES AND HOW DO SAGES APPLY IT WHEN HELPING ASPIRANTS ALONG ON THE INITIATIC PATH? 6. WHY IS IT IMPORTANT FOR SPIRITUAL TEACHERS TO NOT HELP PEOPLE BEYOND THEIR CAPACITY TO BE HELPED? 7. WHY ARE SOME SPECIAL "KEYS" TO UNLOCK CERTAIN MEDITATIVE DISCIPLINES AND PHILOSOPHICAL UNDERSTANDINGS REVEALED TO ASARU LEVEL ASPIRANTS AND NOT TO SHEMS LEVEL ASPIRANTS? 8. WHY IS THE ACCESS TO AN AUTHENTIC SPIRITUAL PRECEPTOR, AND A VIABLE INITIATIC PATH, IMPORTANT FOR POSITIVE SPIRITUAL DEVELOPMENT? 9. OBSTACLES TO BECOMING A QUALIFIED APPLICANT FOR ASAR INITIATION AND DISCIPLINES TO OVERCOME THEM 10. How to Overcome Failure on the Spiritual Path 11. OBSTACLES INCLUDE: 12. DISCIPLINES TO OVERCOME THE OBSTACLES INCLUDE: 13. What criteria are used to evaluate aspirants and how should aspirants conduct themselves in order to develop the qualities necessary for Asaru initiation? [available only as eBOOK] ISBN:978-1-937016-00-5

Music Based on the Prt M Hru and other Kemetic Texts

Available on Compact Disc $14.99 and Audio Cassette $9.99

Adorations to the Goddess

Music for Worship of the Goddess

**NEW Egyptian Yoga Music CD
by Sehu Maa
Ancient Egyptian Music CD**
Instrumental Music played on reproductions of Ancient Egyptian Instruments– Ideal for <u>meditation</u> and reflection on the Divine and for the practice of spiritual programs and <u>Yoga exercise sessions.</u>

©1999 By Muata Ashby
CD $14.99 –

MERIT'S INSPIRATION
**NEW Egyptian Yoga Music CD
by Sehu Maa
Ancient Egyptian Music CD**
Instrumental Music played on reproductions of Ancient Egyptian Instruments– Ideal for <u>meditation</u> and reflection on the Divine and for the practice of spiritual programs and <u>Yoga exercise sessions.</u>
©1999 By
Muata Ashby
CD $14.99 –
UPC# 761527100429

ANORATIONS TO RA AND HETHERU
**NEW Egyptian Yoga Music CD
By Sehu Maa (Muata Ashby)
Based on the Words of Power of Ra and HetHeru**
played on reproductions of Ancient Egyptian Instruments **Ancient Egyptian Instruments used: Voice, Clapping, Nefer Lute, Tar Drum, Sistrums, Cymbals** – The Chants, Devotions, Rhythms and Festive Songs Of the Neteru – Ideal for meditation, and devotional singing and dancing.
©1999 By Muata Ashby
CD $14.99 –
UPC# 761527100221

SONGS TO ASAR ASET AND HERU
NEW
Egyptian Yoga Music CD
By Sehu Maa

played on reproductions of Ancient Egyptian Instruments– The Chants, Devotions, Rhythms and Festive Songs Of the Neteru - Ideal for meditation, and devotional singing and dancing.

Based on the Words of Power of Asar (Asar), Aset (Aset) and Heru (Heru) Om Asar Aset Heru is the third in a series of musical explorations of the Kemetic (Ancient Egyptian) tradition of music. Its ideas are based on the Ancient Egyptian Religion of Asar, Aset and Heru and it is designed for listening, meditation and worship. ©1999 By Muata Ashby

CD $14.99 –
UPC# 761527100122

HAARI OM: ANCIENT EGYPT MEETS INDIA IN MUSIC
NEW Music CD
By Sehu Maa

The Chants, Devotions, Rhythms and Festive Songs Of the Ancient Egypt and India, harmonized and played on reproductions of ancient instruments along with modern instruments and beats. Ideal for meditation, and devotional singing and dancing.

Haari Om is the fourth in a series of musical explorations of the Kemetic (Ancient Egyptian) and Indian traditions of music, chanting and devotional spiritual practice. Its ideas are based on the Ancient Egyptian Yoga spirituality and Indian Yoga spirituality.

©1999 By Muata Ashby
CD $14.99 –
UPC# 761527100528

RA AKHU: THE GLORIOUS LIGHT
NEW
Egyptian Yoga Music CD
By Sehu Maa

The fifth collection of original music compositions based on the Teachings and Words of The Trinity, the God Asar and the Goddess Nebethet, the Divinity Aten, the God Heru, and the Special Meditation Hekau or Words of Power of Ra from the Ancient Egyptian Tomb of Seti I and more... played on reproductions of Ancient Egyptian Instruments and modern instruments - Ancient Egyptian Instruments used: Voice, Clapping, Nefer Lute, Tar Drum, Sistrums, Cymbals
– The Chants, Devotions, Rhythms and Festive Songs Of the Neteru – Ideal for meditation, and devotional singing and dancing.

©1999 By Muata Ashby
CD $14.99 –
UPC# 761527100825

GLORIES OF THE DIVINE MOTHER
Based on the hieroglyphic text of the worship of Goddess Net.
The Glories of The Great Mother
©2000 Muata Ashby
CD $14.99 UPC# 761527101129`

MAIN VIDEOS

Egyptian Yoga Exercise Class Level 1
Muata Ashby (Writer), Muata Ashby (Producer), Muata Ashby (Director)

List Price: $25.00
80 minutes, NTSC
UPC: 883629024394
Discover the practice of Egyptian Yoga postures based on the posture system practiced by the Ancient Egyptian priests and priestesses of Ancient Egypt. This is a practice for physical health but also for mental mythological and spiritual journey to higher consciousness.

Introduction to Ancient Egyptian Hieroglyphs
Muata Ashby (Writer), Muata Ashby (Producer), Muata Ashby (Director)

List Price: $25.00
60 minutes, NTSC
UPC: 883629113227
Introduction to Ancient Egyptian Hieroglyphs Class 1

Introduction to Egyptian Yoga
Muata Ashby (Writer), Muata Ashby (Producer), Muata Ashby (Director)

List Price: $25.00
60 minutes, NTSC
UPC: 883629113159
Introduction to Egyptian Yoga philosophy and its influence on other world religions as well as its implications for spiritual evolution as conceived by the Ancient Egyptian sages Lecture by Dr. Muata Ashby

Glorious Light Meditation System of Ancient Egypt
Muata Ashby (Writer), Muata Ashby (Producer), Muata Ashby (Director)

List Price: $25.00
60 minutes, NTSC
UPC: 883629113104
Glorious Light Meditation System of Ancient Egypt is the oldest practice of formal meditation before Buddhism, Hinduism and Taoism. Ra Akhu, the glorious light was commissioned by the Pharaoh Sety 1 and it was enjoined for men and women to practice. This DVD is an introduction to the system and a practice session.

Asarian Resurrection: Myth of Asar, Aset and Heru (Osiris, Isis and Horus)
Muata Ashby (Writer), Muata Ashby (Producer), Muata Ashby (Director)

List Price: $25.00
60 minutes, NTSC
UPC: 883629111247
Audiovisual lecture by Dr. Muata Ashby on the most important myth of ancient Egypt based on the myth of Osiris, Isis and Horus, and its spiritual implications for attaining spiritual enlightenment

Ancient Egyptian Music Session Live Performances
Muata Ashby (Writer), Muata Ashby (Producer), Muata Ashby (Director)

List Price: $25.00
60 minutes, NTSC
UPC: 883629113241
Ancient Egyptian Music Session Live Performances using Ancient Egyptian musical instrument reproductions and original lyric from ancient Egyptian hymbs and texts

Introduction to Maat Philosophy
Muata Ashby (Writer), Muata Ashby (Producer), Muata Ashby (Director)

List Price: $25.00
60 minutes, NTSC
UPC: 883629113234
Introduction to Maat Philosophy, the Ancient Egyptan philosophy of social order, justice and truth

Introduction to Shetaut Neter Part 1 -Egyptian Mysteries
Muata Ashby (Writer), Muata Ashby (Producer), Muata Ashby (Director)

List Price: $25.00
60 minutes, NTSC
UPC: 883629113166
Audiovisual with powerpoint presentation on Shetaut Neter philosophy, the Egyptian mysteries, the Ancient Egyptian religious principles of metaphysics and mysticism. Lecture by Dr. Muata Ashby

Pan-Africanism in Light of Maat Philosophy
Muata Ashby (Writer), Muata Ashby (Producer), Muata Ashby (Director)

List Price: $25.00
60 minutes, NTSC
UPC: 883629113173
Pan-Africanism in Light of Maat Philosophy relates to how the concept of seein African culture in its totality relates to the promotion of African political, economic and social wellbeing under African principles of spiritual ethics Lecture by Dr. Muata Ashby

Mythology of the Ancient Egyptian Yoga Postures
Muata Ashby (Writer), Muata Ashby (Producer), Muata Ashby (Director)

List Price: $25.00
60 minutes, NTSC
UPC: 883629113265
Lecture series by Dr. Muata Ashby-Course traces the African Origins of Civilization, Religion and Philosophy. This video traces the origins and development of the Ancient Egyptian Yoga Postures. Contains slide presentation with actual original photos of the original postures from Ancient Egypt.

www.ingramcontent.com/pod-product-compliance
Lightning Source LLC
Chambersburg PA
CBHW071436080526
44587CB00014B/1877